Spain

Spain

SACHEVERELL SITWELL

B. T. BATSFORD LTD LONDON

First published 1950
Fourth impression 1955
Paperback edition 1961

PRINTED AND BOUND IN THE NETHERLANDS BY
THE HOOIBERG PRINTING COMPANY, EPE, FOR THE PUBLISHERS
B. T. BATSFORD LTD
4 FITZHARDINGE STREET, PORTMAN SQUARE, LONDON W. I

To
Luis Bolín

Contents

Acknowledgment

THE Publishers wish to thank the following for permission to reproduce the illustrations included in this book:

Baron Studios for figs 6 and 32; J. Allan Cash, F.R.P.S. for figs 26 and 31; Eric de Maré for figs 7 and 11; A. F. Kersting, F.R.P.S. for figs 1, 2, 13, 20 and 23; the Rev. F. Sumner for fig. 3; Direccion General del Turismo, Madrid for figs 4, 5, 8–10, 14–19, 21, 22, 24, 25 and 27–30.

List of Illustrations

Between pages 32 and 33

1 *Seville: riders at the Fair*
2 *Avila, with the late eleventh-century walls*
3 *Burgos: the west front of the cathedral*
4 *Madrid: Puente de Toledo*
5 *Madrid: Hospicio Provincial*
6 *Granada: The Alhambra – view from Mirador*
7 *Granada: The Alhambra – Court of the Lions*
8 *Granada: The Alhambra – Court of the Lions*

Between pages 80 and 81

9 *Toledo cathedral: El Trasparente*
10 *Segovia: the fifteenth-century castle of Coca*
11 *Ronda: bridge and gorge*
12 *Zamora: the dome of the cathedral*
13 *Toledo cathedral: the west front*
14 *Seville: procession during Holy Week*
15 *History of Tarquin: "Black" Tapestry of Zamora*
16 *Salamanca: Charra costumes*

Between pages 124 and 125

17 *Cuenca*
18 *The lovers of Lagartera*
19 *Santiago de Compostela: façade of El Obradoiro*
20 *Segovia cathedral: the crossing*
21 *Salamanca: costume of La Alberca*
22 *Catalonia: mountain landscape*
23 *Segovia: Roman aqueduct*
24 *Salamanca: Charras from Palencia de Negrilla*

Between pages 172 and 173

25 *Mallorca: the cathedral and harbour of Palma*
26 *Costa Brava: repairing nets at Rosas*
27 *Ansó, Aragon: a church procession*

The photograph on the cover of this book, showing the Court of the Lions in the Alhambra, Granada, was taken by the Keystone Press Agency Limited

Introduction

THIS present work is the fruit and accumulation of many journeys made to Spain. My earliest journey was during March and April 1919, immediately after the end of the First World War. Who that was twenty years old is ever likely to forget his impressions of Toledo and of the paintings of El Greco? At that day, long ago now, the guide books were inadequate and you could walk into any church in Toledo and not know what pictures you would find. And the Escorial? Probably there is no building in the world that makes so personal an impression. And El Greco's *St. Maurice and the Theban Legion*, his masterpiece, and certainly the most extraordinary "Mannerist" painting in the world? Everyone who goes to Spain will see these, as they will the Prado. My next experience of Spain was in 1925, when I went to Barcelona and Valencia, and for the first time to Seville. I spent a month in Seville, and nearly as long in Granada. The following year I went, through Portugal, to Salamanca and Valladolid, and to Burgos. A year later, on the way home from Morocco, to Cádiz, and passing Guadalupe, to Madrid again, and once more to Burgos. Upon other occasions I have been to Catalonia, and three separate times to Santiago de Compostela.

For no land in Europe, probably no other land in the civilized world, has so violent a personality, so strong a flavour, as that of Spain. By contrast, Italy and her cities, Rome, Florence, Venice, come to the foreigner as his second patrimony. Her paintings and architecture, her landscape, are for his pleasure. They were made, or created, with this end in view. That is the virtue and weakness of Italy, and of the Italians. But we may be inclined to think, at first, that Spain is for the Spaniards, and for the Spaniards alone. It will not last. For the Spaniard is deeper and more profound than the Italian. There is no more wonderful description of Italy, in her splendour and decadence, than the passage in the Fourth Book of *The Dunciad*, where Pope sets forth upon an imaginary grand tour of the Italian cities of the arts:

11

"To happy convents, bosomed deep in vines,
Where slumber abbots, purple as their wines:
To isles of fragrance, lily-silvered vales,
Diffusing languor in the panting gales:
To lands of singing, or of dancing slaves,
Love-whisp'ring woods, and lute-resounding waves.
But chief her shrine where naked Venus keeps,
And Cupids ride the lion of the deeps;
Where, eased of fleets, the Adriatic main,
Wafts the smooth eunuch and enamoured swain."

The reading of these lines, if I may be permitted to quote from something I have written before, "is like a magical transition from the hot south up to Venice. Capri and Ischia, isles of fragrance with their cliffs of jonquil and narcissus, are evoked in the same breath as Paestum in its plain of asphodel. The poem, then, seems to move by magical reptation through woods of ilex, as it might be Rome evoked in its seven hills, to the decadence of Venice. That perpetual carnival is portrayed in the degradation of the lion of the deeps, ridden by Cupids and garlanded with flowers, while the venality of its decay is exposed in the shrine of naked Venus. The last couplet of all is a miraculous image of decrepitude, bringing, as it does, the tainted waters of the Bosphorus to lap the marble quays of Venice, the gliding caique is transposed for the gondola; and then, in the next instance, the voice of Senesino, or Egiziello, seem to sound, though never named, upon the waters. Indeed, after this, there is nothing more to be said about Venice in its decadence. All, all is in that final couplet."

But with Spain, and the Spaniards, it is another matter. They have never become, like the Italians, the slaves of their own music, so that the opera singer and the organ grinder are typical of their race. The fierce and terrible integrity of the Spaniards has enabled them to survive the horrors of their Civil War, which, singly, was one of the worst disasters which has befallen any country of the modern world. Their losses, be it remembered, were, proportionately, double what we suf-

12

fered in the First World War. It would be true, perhaps, to say that the Spaniards are the slaves of their own history. And it is a proud history, prodigal in pride of deeds and names, fertilizing, in course of that, half of the continent of America. But, also, the Spaniards have been the greatest builders after the Romans. The Spanish cathedrals, and not only Toledo, Seville, Burgos, Compostela, but a host of lesser ones, including many of which the ordinary reader may scarcely know the names, are unparalleled, not for the stone vessels alone, but for the extraordinary nature and richness of their contents. It has been attempted in this book to write more of these, and of the landscape of Spain, than of the Prado. For El Greco, Velázquez, Goya are, by now, the commonplace of all persons who are ever likely to look into these pages. Having been the author of one of the first books in the English language to illustrate the paintings of El Greco, I feel it will not be laid to my charge that I have neglected him. But, in fact, El Greco is not so typical of Spain as even some Spaniards would have us think. Velázquez is the real Spaniard, and *Las Meninas*, now shown in a room to itself in the Prado, is one of the miracles of European painting. I am not the uncritical, indiscriminate admirer of Goya, neither can I see in him, as some critics profess to do, the prophet of the century of "the common man". To my personal tastes the Goya room in the Prado is ever something of a disappointment. I have my own explanation to offer of his huge group of Carlos IV and the Royal Family, which is that, like many another great painter before and after him, Goya could not "bring off" his picture, could not make a success of it, and therefore continued it partly to amuse the Royal family in question. I do not believe it is the last and supreme satire upon monarchy that it is supposed to be. Goya is the great master in his drawings and etchings, and in a few of his portraits. The *Condesa de Chinchón* is probably his masterpiece. I find his cartoons for tapestry more wooden, and less lively, than their reputation. I gather an almost equal pleasure from the despised Bayeu and Maella, if it be that sort of Goya that we are admiring; while there is a lesser master, Paret y Alcázar (his small picture of Carlos III being

13

served with dinner in some tapestried corner of a palace is one of the little discoveries of the Prado), at the same time that the "costume" portraits of Raphael Mengs and of the "early Victorian" Vicente López are not to be ignored. But, indeed, the whole history of a country is in the Prado, as in no other gallery. The Accadémia does not tell us so much of Venice, the Uffizi of Florence, as the Prado does of Spain. But I have had to resist the temptation, one fraught with danger to some-one of my temperament, to write of Spain as though it was the Kingdom of the Habsburg and the Bourbon.

Instead, it has been my attempt to proceed from province to province of the entire country dealing with its monuments in turn, and with no particular emphasis upon their date and style. In this way I believe that no building of any importance has been neglected, except the Escorial, of which I have at-tempted no description because it is part of universal know-ledge, and is still, as from the day of its construction, an eighth wonder of the world. Herrera is, in consequence, perhaps the only one of the great architects who is not discussed. I have attempted, also, to set the buildings in the landscape, and where appropriate have described the local festivals and cos-tume. Perhaps an author fortunate enough to know Italy well is, by that, the better equipped to write of Spain. What I hope will emerge from these pages, as though of instinct, is the unvarying kindness and good nature of the Spaniards. They have not been treated so well by the post-war world that one has the right to expect this, but they are always, and uni-versally, polite and courteous to the Englishman. The Span-iards, it to be remarked, do not change sides in the middle of a war, and their hands are not stained with the blood of many thousands of our countrymen who, of tradition, were their friends. The Spaniards are a proud race, better left alone, but who excel themselves in kindness to the foreigner, once they know him. Were I to mention friendly Spaniards, by name, it would be a list of all the Spaniards I have met. But my In-troduction, as though in anticipation, is hurrying to its end. And I would not stop it. For we are on our way to *las Fiestas de Sevilla* and stop for a drink of orange juice and iced water at an inn beside the road. The blue geranium is in flower at the foot of the wall, and there is nothing else for miles in any direction but the high plateau and the snowy *sierra* in the distance:

> "It was so hot
> That when we got out at the Albergue
> I saw the ghosts of white and blue irises
> Against the whitewashed wall
> Where there were no flowers at all.
> Outside the town
> In the sunset
> The cave dwellers, the troglodytes,
> Were sunning themselves in the doorways of their caves;
> It was the first hot day after the iron winter."

The Feria of Seville glitters, in the distance, with its lights and music. We are on our way.

1

Andalucía

1. FERIA

Crossing the Frontier – San Sebastián – Burgos – The Feria

THE writer upon Spain – and his companion, who is the
reader – have so huge a kingdom lying before them and one
that shines and beckons with so many fair prospects and rich
prizes that in order to miss nothing of its peculiar and instant
individuality we present ourselves in the old manner, proceed-
ing along the earth's surface and not in an aeroplane above it,
and appear with due formality at the Spanish frontier. It is a
long way south of Paris before the vines begin: no more, at first,
than a few rows an inch or two high, more like gnarled and
twisted wooden nails, with no promise of the trellis and the
tented shade; but by the afternoon we had reached Touraine,
that province of hills, wide rivers, and restored or sham castles. Next day, after the long monotony of the Landes, we
were over the Spanish frontier, and a blue jacaranda tree
was in full flower upon the way to San Sebastián.

There can be no country in the world that is so soon itself
once you have crossed the border, in this instance the bridge
over the Bidassoa. Not so much, though, in virtue of the landscape as of its inhabitants. For if you arrive in Spain by way
of Irún and San Sebastián the green valleys are not, at first,
so far different from those upon the French side of the Pyrenees. There are the same Basque châlets with wooden balconies and overhanging eaves, and big boulders to weigh down
the roofs. Tall, cliff-like apartment houses border the narrow
mountain streams, for we are nearing San Sebastián through
many suburbs, over a river, and down past the shops to La
Concha, the miniature child's bay of San Sebastián – with Monte Urgull at one end, the island of Santa Clara in the middle,

and a promenade all along the water's edge below the white hotels, a promenade planted with a double row of tamarisks clipped into the shape of parasols, and a bay far more like Derain's painted back-cloth for *La Boutique Fantasque*, intended for the harbour of Nice in the days of the early paddle steamers, than any other seaside town that we have ever seen. San Sebastián has still something of that air clinging to it which must have pervaded Biarritz during the reign of the Empress Eugénie, both in and out of season, and deriving from its patronage by rich Spaniards and South Americans. Coming from England, we notice the *chocolatiers* and the shops for gloves and shoes. Up in the old part of the town, at the foot of Monte Urgull, there is a church with a Baroque façade fronting the narrow street that leads to it, a theatre piece, for it is that in effect, foretaste of the warm scene-painter's architecture of Valencia and the Levante. This could only be the work of a Spaniard. But except for the famous Restaurant Nicolasa there is nothing more in San Sebastián, a watering place that until a few years ago had been, in the words of the French guide book, "le séjour d'été de la Cour d'Espagne".

At least, and at any rate, we are in Spain. But the problem now comes, as though in liberty of her hills and plains, of where to go. For supposing you have stayed the night in San Sebastián, there are many and various directions open to you in the morning. You could go along the Basque coast, past Santander, to Santillana del Mar, one of the loveliest little towns in Spain, with its small palaces or *casas solariegas*, and their huge coats-of-arms; or in the other direction to Pamplona and down along the Pyrenees. Or straight ahead and to Madrid, which is our choice, though we resolve in the impetuosity bred of our release from the snows of winter to continue straight through the capital to Seville. Spaniards have a saying that the true Spain only begins at Vitoria, seventy or eighty miles inland and about a quarter of the way between the frontier and the capital of Spain. When we get to Vitoria we shall be, so to speak, upon the Spanish mainland, among troglodyte cliffs and making for Mercutio's "dew-dropping

18

South", for aloes and prickly pears, where, if we believe Ford – and he still rings true – we shall find "the dark daughters of Moultan sitting in their rags under the vines".

So straight away to Vitoria, which, is, indeed, a pleasant little town. A fine Sunday morning when we arrive there, with a band playing in the Paseo de la Florida, "beaux ombrages, statues, fontaines", as the guide prophesies, and it comes to pass. But for the rest this leafy town came into history in the Napoleonic wars, when it was the scene of Wellington's victory over Joseph Bonaparte, who left eight thousand of his polyglot army dead upon the field, abandoned his pictures and treasure, and soon afterwards was driven out of Spain. Vitoria was, also, a place of importance in the two Carlist wars, those seeming Spanish anachronisms of the nineteenth century, to the terrible but picturesque nature of which we must pay due attention if we want to understand the character of the Spaniards and of Spain. Not now, but later; for we must press on with our journey. Some time before reaching Vitoria we have come out from the green valleys into the high Spanish plain, and about half-way between Vitoria and Burgos we enter Old Castile. Monotonous the landscape may be, but it is the most magnificent monotony in the whole world. The wonders of this huge tableland, broken by snow-capped mountains, presenting the aspect of so many burnt up, excoriated lunar landscapes over the rims of which, so vast is their scale, we crawl by road or in the train; or waving green cornlands; or a wintry, rainlogged desert; but for the most part lying out into illimitable distance with the barest simplicity of outline; these wonders would need many generations of human experience to assimilate and explain. It is, in fact, not monotonous at all, unless there be monotony and sameness in mountain, cloud, and monolith, but, at this present, the road leads ahead into infinity and we are climbing steadily, higher and higher, into Old Castile.

And it is Sunday morning still, or rather, the hour has drifted on into afternoon, and by the time the bluebell spires of Burgos (they are the golden dried husks and not the living flowers) are to be seen far away coming out of the plain it is

19

so late as to rouse apprehension as to the possibility of lunch-eon. Half-past three, or nearer four o'clock, but here in Spain there is no need to hurry. Previous visits during twenty-five years, or longer, which on occasion had necessitated the spend-ing of several nights in discomfort and misery, left no pleas-ant anticipation of the hotels in Burgos, but there is a new hotel with a dining-room in Castilian style full at that late hour of travellers and citizens just settling down to luncheon. Upon the way to the hotel through the narrow twisting streets we came to the oddly shaped, arcaded Plaza Mayor, so typical of a Spanish town, with statue of Carlos III in the centre, in whose goat-like features, being nostalgically inclined and un-able to forget early and old experience, we may catch an echo of the palace of Caserta and the Bay of Naples.[1] In the hotel there were excellent *langostinos*, Spanish olives and anchovies in hot pastry, followed by a *tortilla*, and much else besides. The frescoed dining-room, unpretentious and agree-able, was in the vernacular Spanish style, double agreeable after the international hotels of San Sebastián. And this is as it shoud be; for Burgos after its fashion is the most Spanish town in Spain, a statement which will be furiously contradict-ed by those persons who possess their own ideas and theories as to what is Spain and what is Spanish; and I do not say that Burgos is my own favourite, my personal tastes run, perhaps, to quite different extremes and other manners, but it will not be denied that for a certain kind of flamboyant late Gothic, entirely unlike our own contemporary Perpendicular, Burgos is a city without rival in the world. In point of architecture this is in a sense the indigenous speech of Spain, though com-pound of foreign verbs and particles, so that in order to treat of it as it deserves we resume all our impressions of Burgos into one, and for the sake of freshness and clearness of outline are to imagine that we are seeing the capital of Old Castile for the first time. Let it, also, be the first occasion on which we are entering a Spanish cathedral and the first building typ-ically Spanish that we have met in Spain.

[1] Carlos III was King of the Two Sicilies (1734–1759) before succeeding to the throne of Spain (1759–1788).

This most profuse and elaborate of Spanish cathedrals, with its twin spires of open stonework and its octagonal central lantern flowering into eight more floreated and pointed turrets, has been built into the steep slope of a hill as though for semi-protection or in order to take root there. The pair of great spires are cusped and ornamented and have a curious analogy to the masts of medieval ships, particularly in the look-out balconies just below their summits, the effect of the thick stone trellis or diaper in which the spires are encased being to suggest that this is in order to protect the mast-poles from being snapped or broken. But this entire upper ornamentation of the exterior is of German origin. The plan of the cathedral, however, is French, and underneath all the ornamentation it is a great thirteenth-century French church, which explains our remark that the speech of the Spaniards in architecture is full of foreign verbs and particles. Burgos cathedral, we say in conclusion before plunging into its chill interior, is not impressively mammoth-like in dimension: rather it is small compared with other ecclesiastical monsters, and entirely overlaid, inside and out, with ornament.

The interior could not be more demonstrably and undeniably Spanish or more typical of Spain. Those persons who have seen nothing of the sort before will be amazed at the superb ironwork, the towering wrought iron screens and grills, or *rejas,* and at the railed-in processional way leading from the choir to the high altar. The *coro* itself, with its hundred and more carved stalls of box and walnut and its great lecterns and illuminated choir books, resembles as ever a musty old music room and library in one. At the far or east end of the cathedral, behind its own *reja* or wrought iron railing, lies the chapel of the Condestable, or to give but his bare name and two of his titles, Don Pedro Hernández de Velasco, Conde de Haro and Hereditary Constable of Castile. The double tomb of this nobleman and his wife, Doña Mencía de Mendoza, of Carrara marble carved by a sculptor from Genoa, though fine and splendid, is perhaps hardly worthy of so extravagant a chapel in this land of tombs. It is the work of Hans and Simon of Cologne, father and son, the German ar-

21

chitects who built the central lantern of the cathedral and the twin open spires, and all the panoply of Spanish heraldry is displayed upon the walls. There are pages, in pairs, holding up shields-of-arms, and lions erect on their hind legs, so curled and glossy of mane that they resemble living golden fleeces, and so high upon the wall that all we can distinguish is that they are holding stone cartwheels enclosing sacred initials or monograms in their front paws. High over our heads is the open-traceried, eight-pointed star-vault or *cimborrio* of the ceiling, a design not unlike a white passion flower or clematis from the blanched colour of the stone.

But there is more to see in the cathedral. The chapel of the Condestable has its own sacristy and treasury; and a beadle in a gown of green velvet will unlock room after room along the cloisters. The silks and brocades, the silver pyxes and monstrances, massy plate, coral ornaments, jewelled necklaces, carved ivories, and precious stones of a Spanish cathedral will daze and bewilder the eyes. There are but few kinds of sightseeing so rewarding, and withal so tiring, as these earliest attempts at museum arrangement in the modern world. It is better, perhaps, to save our energies for the chapel of Santa Tecla, with its *media naranja* (half-orange) dome treated with polychrome decorations applied to the stone ground, and the work of a member of the Churriguera family. This is a quiet and modest example of the exuberant style that spread to Mexico. It is tactful to its setting in this Gothic cathedral, but interests by reason of the wild and unprecedented units or motifs of its ornament. Perhaps the polyglot character and history of this typically and supremely Spanish cathedral are now apparent.

Hans and Simon of Cologne, who must have settled the cathedral on its course of ornament, had a number of craftsmen, workers in metal and carvers in wood and stone, to carry out the details, and it was work which extended over two or three generations. Among them were Germans and Burgundians. But we have still to see the *escalera dorada*, a double staircase with gilded balusters by a French ironsmith, that descends into the body of the north transept from the slope of the hill outside and is the work of Diego de Silóee. The stair is an architectural conceit serving no useful purpose, but more must be said about this individual with the odd surname, and about his father, Gil de Silóee, who was one of the very greatest of the wandering artists of the later Middle Ages.

In order to establish his curious identity we have to return for a moment to Hans of Cologne, the architect of the twin spires and of the lantern, for he was brought to Spain by a Jewish bishop of Burgos, Alonso de Cartagena.[1] It appears that Gil de Silóee, as well as Hans of Cologne, owed his arrival in Spain to Alonso de Cartagena, who had been born a Jew, and that Gil de Silóee himself was a Jew, for his father was a merchant of Nuremberg called Samuel and his mother's name was Miriam, in the light of which knowledge it may be wondered whether Hans of Cologne was not Jewish also. In the second generation Diego de Silóee certainly, and it is probable Simon of Cologne, were born in Burgos, and in the instance of the Silóees, father and son, we have the only considerable artists of Jewish origin to appear in Europe before the twentieth century, and with Gil de Silóee, it may be, the greatest artist in the plastic arts that the Jewish race has produced. This, too, in that short interregnum before the Jews with the Moors were expelled from Spain; but if, as could be advanced with some little force of probability, Hans of Cologne, his son Simon, and grandson Francisco, were Jews also, then the work of these two families becomes, perhaps, more interesting even than their skill deserves and we have to look at Burgos cathedral in the light of that ambiguous origin and it becomes something unique, indeed, in Christian annals.

But Gil de Silóee has to be seen at the Cartuja de Miraflores, two or three miles outside Burgos, a royal foundation built by Hans and Simon of Cologne. The chapel is contemporary with Eton College chapel and the chapel of King's Col-

[1] A previous bishop of Burgos, it may be added, was Pablo de Santa María, a Jew who had been married to a Jewess in early life and was not baptized a Christian till he was forty years old. They had a son, Gonzalvo, who was made bishop of Sigüenza.

lege, Cambridge, to the former of which, save that it is built of
golden not of grey stone, its exterior bears a certain resemblance, and it contains the tomb of Don Juan II and Isabella
of Portugal, whose grandmother was the Plantagenet Phil-
ippa of Lancaster, daughter of John of Gaunt. The tomb is
a marble octagon; in fact, it is eight-pointed like the great
lantern or *cimborrio* of the cathedral or the eight-pointed
passion flower or clematis of the chapel of the Condestable. It
is, therefore, sixteen-sided, with the king and his queen lying
with crowned heads, in robes of incredible richness, the Queen
holding an open prayer-book in her hand, the cornices and
sides of this star octagon being ornamented with allegorical
figures of prophets and evangelists, with two lions each to the
eight main angles, sixteen in all, upholding coats-of-arms, and
carvings of birds and quadrupeds, of leaves and branches.[1]
You can climb some wooden steps and look down over the
wrought iron railings upon this pair of effigies. They are,
indeed, most beautiful, not least in the back of the wimple of
the Queen's headdress, the handling of which, now, seems to
us unlike any other work of the Middle Ages, due perhaps to
the pent-up imagery in Gil de Silóee because of his Eastern
blood. We can only repeat our previous conviction, stated in another place, that this king and queen lying, crown on head, in
robes of ceremony, form the most entire masterpiece of late
Gothic sculpture, and that for its special qualities there is
nothing to equal it in other lands. Even persons of the most
levelling political tendencies must be awed and silenced by this
witness to the splendours and miseries of old Spain. Upon the
wall opposite is the wall tomb, also by Gil de Silóee, of the young
Infante Alfonso, at whose early death the future Queen Isabella became heiress to the throne. The Infante is kneeling at a
prie-dieu under an elaborate arched canopy, and at the sides
there are carvings of children playing in the tendrils of a vine
and picking grapes. The astonishing golden complexity and
elaboration of the *retablo* rising behind the high altar is also
by the same sculptor. Like many another Spanish *retablo*, it

[1] The plan of the tomb is a square superimposed upon a square, a
design which is a Moorish pattern.

24

sparkles and glitters with the gold of Mexico, and if this be the first *retablo* to be seen we may carry away little more than the impression of the crucifix and of the figure of a pelican feeding its young with its own blood. All of these monuments, these tombs and this *retablo,* are due to Isabel la Católica and to the new-found wealth of Spain. But it is time to come out of the chapel of the Cartuja into the golden sunset, and by way once more of the crockets and pinnacles of Burgos, its late Gothic buildings in the failing light as prolix and repetitive of ornament as a wood of bluebells, we arrived after many hours at the capital, nearly in the middle of the night.

A light grey rain was falling a day or two later when we left Madrid, not so much falling perhaps as implicit or suspended in the lead-grey air. It had been tropically hot for the time of year, hot enough to have luncheon and dinner out of doors in the garden of the hotel, a little oasis of white columns, of palms and pine trees, surrounded on three sides by trams, but where an owl hooted late at night when the trams were intermittent and the jazz-band had done. The road out of Madrid starts from the Puente de Toledo, one of the most fantastic and magnificent creations of decadent architecture, a bridge that is splendid and Spanish in scale but positively Aztec in ornament, and that could lead over the lagoons, the *chinampas,* or floating gardens, to the stepped pyramids and to Montezuma's palace. At one time it traversed a dreary slum of new tenements and shacks built out of petrol tins. Later comes Aranjuez and its green groves, its splashing waters and its nightingales. The treeless plain resumes; and presently, under a bluer sky, we reach the deep red soil and the vineyards of Manzanares, where, in the words of Richard Ford, "the red blood of the vine issues from this valley of stones". We are in the midst of La Mancha, among the bare hills and windmills of Cervantes. Next comes Valdepeñas, with more vineyards and a still redder soil. There follow a rocky gorge and the mountains of the Sierra Morena. The rock-rose is in flower upon the hillside, first one and then hundreds of white rock-roses, as far as the eyes can see, and the rarer crimson-pink or it may be magenta. Lower down,

25

as we near the plain, there are asphodels and soon dwarf palm (palmito), the acanthus, and the aspidistra. A huge peony, alone of its kind, is in flower down in the valley. The first cactuses and prickly pears appear. This is Andalucía. Is it only in imagination that there seems to be a mist or haze out of Africa hinging over the plain? But the heat is deep and tremendous. The sky is unfathomable and of intense blue. When we stop late in the afternoon at the Albergue de Bailén, and the blue flags are in flower, the sun awnings are let down to shade the whitewashed pillars and the semicircular dining-room is cool though full of travellers bound, like ourselves, for *las fiestas de Sevilla*.

Some hours later we are in the suburbs of Córdoba, and coming to the Roman bridge over the Guadalquivir turn aside up the little hill to the battlemented walls of the cathedral or, we would have it, the mosque, la Mezquita, as it is still called today. It is late, nearly dark, and the doors are locked; but one gate is yet open into the court of orange trees, and the lovely, spicy, drowsy smell of the orange blossom, after all that has happened during these many years of war, is an intoxication and a draught of magic. In that moment one felt that one might not have lived to know that scent again. Impossible not to stand quite still and motionless and breathe it in. A pyramid of the red-gold fruit lies heaped in a corner under a Moorish archway. It was worth while coming all the way from London in order to breathe for this one instant in the orange grove. And the mosque was opened for us, which looked, in that darkening hour, even more beautiful and mysterious than I had remembered it. But a mosque that is ten centuries old must not be hurried. We leave its forest of columns and horseshoe arches, the Moorish stalactites and honeycells, for another time, and crossing the bridge with its many arches stop for petrol by an age-old water well, a fountain to which the women come with their pitchers, where horses and mules are watered now that dark has fallen, where not so long ago, when the women were veiled, there must have been men in gowns and turbans, and long strings of camels. For that is the secret of the orange blossom. Those are perfumes of Arabia. And for a couple of hours more, through the night, there came that breath of orange blossom from time to time and the deep croaking of the frogs. The "dew-dropping South" of Mercutio was eternal and unaltered; and so it continued, balmy and spice-laden out of the dark leaves, until the red glare of a distant town announced Seville; and after enquiry in the dusty suburbs we drove past the fair ground, with its high masts and arc lamps, and along the flank of the famous Tobacco Factory, no longer used for that purpose, to where the hotel, with innumerable motorcars drawing up and departing, stood enmeshed, as it were, in a perfect cocoon of tramlines.

To awaken in Seville is, in itself, something of a sensation, as though the syllables of that magical name had been ringing in one's ears, through all the other noises, all night long. And coming out of the hotel how hot it was! How narrow the pavement! How shrill the motorhorns and the clanging of the trams. But here was the cathedral, its golden parapets stained with lichen or even nodding with weeds in that cloudless sky. And in a moment or two we are in the Plaza de San Fernando, where formerly, in the cloisters of the Franciscan convent, stood the Roman statue of the *Comendador* in his toga, in fact the statue of the supper scene in *Don Giovanni*. Since last I saw Seville this square of San Fernando has been converted into the most beautiful of rose gardens. The rose bushes in the middle of April were in full bloom, a most wonderful vision after the long and pitiless winter, roses high and low and in every variety of form and colour, some few of them, no doubt, new triumphs of Señor Pedro Dot and the rosarians of Catalonia, and many of them more scented than the new English roses. They were beautiful in full sun and not less lovely when the rose beds were in shade under the tall palms.

But, continuing on our way, where is there a street of shops more fascinating than the Sierpes, as narrow as the Mercería in Venice and, like that, motorless, without wheeled traffic, but so much more interesting than the Mercería owing to the goods in the shop windows: the high tortoiseshell combs and mantillas, and fans painted with scenes of bull fights and

27

serenades or the processions of Holy Week, with farther on the posters of bull fights and coloured postcards of matadors in the tobacconists' shops, the confectioner at the far end of the Sierpes with the bonbon boxes in his window formed in the shape of the cowled figures of the different *cofradías* of the Semana Santa; at about which spot in the Sierpes, towards noon, are gathered the *aficionados* of the bull ring in their short jackets, stiff-brimmed Córdoban hats, black or grey, and carrying their long, thin sticks or wands, sticks which are peeled of their bark in alternate rings of black and white, tapering to a point, and with a forked end where they rest their thumbs. The *majos*, or most of them, are countrymen come into Seville for the bull fights, and they are meeting their friends at the wineshops in the Sierpes, a sign that it is midday and that soon the shop shutters will be noisily let down.

At the hotel a mule carriage and pair was waiting at the door, for its owner had come to call upon us, and it was in this same carriage, with its coachman and footman on the box in grey Córdoban hats and liveries of grey cloth with brown facings, that later in the evening, after a long and necessary siesta, we drove through the Parque de María Luisa and down the Paseo de las Delicias, names that breathe or whisper of the tall acacias, the roses, camellias, and orange trees, of what must be the most beautiful public park in Europe. Indeed, this drive becomes in memory one of the most lovely experiences I have had for many years, not least because of the anachronism of the mule team, not an anachronism really, because there were few other vehicles but mule- or horse-drawn carriages, but there was an indescribable air of excitement even down the languorous and scented avenues, a hurrying in one direction; and here we saw the first of the many horsemen of the Feria, but forbear to describe them, because, as warned at the time, they will appear in all their finery tomorrow. The Paseo de las Delicias, which lies along the bank of the Guadalquivir, now comes out from the shade of its trees into a huge plain, known, appropriately, as the Tablada, and we see the scene towards which all this concourse of persons has been riding or driving, the whitewashed walls and enclosures of the Venta de Antequera.

For it is the eve of the Feria of Seville and the great festivities will begin tomorrow. The fighting bulls have been driven in this morning, or the night before, from the *ganaderías* and are now penned or paddocked, each enclosure bearing the breeder's name above it. Thirty or forty bulls, enough for a week's entertainment, are in the three or four enclosures, each with a bullock or two, a cowbell round its neck, for company, and in order to avoid monotony. The huge beasts are coloured either black or brown and seem hardly conscious of the great crowd come to watch them. To the stranger they may look alike, but the *aficionados* can discuss their heredity not only in physical appearance but in movement and action. The strains of the different breeders have their qualities and peculiarities and are known for their particular temperaments and methods of attack, in light of which they are being examined by the onlookers for their physical condition, while the ignorant majority are only come to look at each other and at the animals that are doomed to die.

It is the Venta, in a sense the first of the ceremonies of the Feria, and the grandstand above the pens is crowded with the rank and fashion of Madrid and Seville, drinking sherry or eating ices to the strains of a band. Young men and women on horseback, in Andalucian costume – but it is even painful to stare at them in the direct rays of the setting sun – are pressing their way through the crowd. Many will stay and dine here, and look down on the bulls that are lying out like shadows in a false moonlight; but we drive back along the Paseo de las Delicias into Seville behind the jangling mule team. The sun is setting, the church bells are ringing; tomorrow will be the Feria.

It has been settled that at midday we are to drive round the fairground. The mule carriage is at the door, but today both grooms and mules are in their splendour: blue and yellow cords and cockades (the colours of the owner); rosettes of blue and yellow on the trappings and the harness; blue and yellow hammercloths; while our host himself has put on a grey Córdoban hat for the occasion. And so, along the length of the Tobacco Factory, with its Baroque statues trumpeting fame upon the skyline, to the Feria. The fairground is nearby, on the Prado de San Sebastián, but "it is not so much a fair as an outing or festival", lasting three days, and in which the entire population, high and low, participate. A huge cattle fair is the immediate excuse for the Feria, and for the centenary year, the celebrations have been doubled and extended to six days, with a bull fight every afternoon. Passing the fountains, which will be illuminated this evening, the scene of the Feria is a quadruple avenue, three or four hundred yards long, and bordered on both sides of its four lengths with *casetas*, which are pavilions or open summer-houses, "the origin of which is to be traced to the tents put up by the cattle dealers, long ago, in order to sleep beside their herds". No motorcars are allowed upon the two middle avenues, which are only open for carriages and persons on horseback.

Within a moment our mule carriage is moving no quicker than at walking pace. The heat is tremendous, such as it may have been seventy or eighty years ago in Hyde Park or the Champs Elysées during the age of the carriage and the crinoline at the height of summer, and such as I do not remember, of its kind, since childhood, since in fact I last drove among the other carriages on Sunday morning along the Esplanade. I believe this must be the sensation of all persons who see the Feria for the first time, as we did, at midday, when the great concourse of persons is driving or riding round. We shall discover that it is due, principally, to the Gypsy dresses worn by the young women. It is this that makes the scene like a vision of the early or middle part of the last century, though it is only necessary to be reminded of the riders or the mule carriages to know that it has nothing to do with that dead world of the Bois de Boulogne or Rotten Row. For this is a sight that is to be seen nowhere else in the world today; and it must be described slowly and, as it were, at walking pace.

There are many different sorts of dresses. All are not dressed alike. The young women of the sidewalks are wearing flounced skirts that touch the ground, of blue or pink or red cotton,

30

patterned with different sizes of white dots. All day, yesterday, we had noticed such dresses being carried home from the dressmakers, over one arm of an owner or dressmaker, and had stopped and tried to examine them. It was a revelation of how many effects can be made with a white ring or circle. But there are dresses of white flounces too, edged with a blue or red cording, like the moonlit equivalent to those patterns of mock suns. And, as well, there are the different shapes and forms of flounces, crinolines, if we call them that, of three or four or five or more tiers or storeys. The young women in these full skirts walk bareheaded, with a scarf or handkerchief at their necks, their glossy hair kept well in place, always with the traditional flower behind the ear. There are little girls of three or four years old dressed in even more detail than their cousins or elder sisters; sometimes with a long train behind that sweeps the ground. And we are looking continually, delighted at every turn, for fresh ideas and colours, as for instance to see a green dress or one of saffron yellow, which did not happen till the third morning of the Feria, when a flowered crinoline of daffodil yellow made an appearance, was lost in the crowd, but quickly recognized again.

At this hour of the morning the *casetas* are half empty. The crowd is on foot or on horseback. Upon the pair of outer avenues, where it is allowed, we even pass motorcars carrying three or four young girls draped in their full skirts upon the bonnet and the mudguards. But this is in bad taste. It is one of the few faults of the Feria, and is corrected, quickly, by much jangling and a mule carriage of more substantial make, drawn by a "six-in-hand", with a middle-aged man in short black coat and Córdoban hat holding the reins. This beautiful equipage seems to sail forward upon the admiring glances of the onlookers. But, rounding the corner, we are on the outer side of our avenue and can see in every detail the splendid cavaliers and their ladies as they ride towards us and pass by. Taking the young women first, there are the two sorts, those who go pillion and those who ride alone. The pillion riders, perched precariously with an arm round their partner's waist or holding to the horse's tail, wear the flounced skirts of the pedestri-

31

ans. Their brothers, or lovers, ride generally one arm akimbo, which accentuates their thin waists. Many are wearing elaborate and fanciful leather trousers, in which we can see the origin of the cowboys' leggings and of the Mexican *charro* costume. The young women ride pillion with an amazing grace, the beauty of their bare heads and arms in that violent sunlight being as animal as the steeds they share. Every young woman is beautiful to look at, some of the girls being real visions of Spanish beauty with their camellia skins and black hair and eyes. But not all are dark, and there are young girls riding pillion, in green or white crinolines, with fair hair, bareheaded like the rest, and glowing in the midday sun.

It is wonderful to watch a cavalier, arm akimbo, riding towards us, Spanish-fashion, and then to wait and admire the young woman upon the crupper holding lightly to his waist. But the other sort of riders, the true Amazons, are yet more enthralling, those who ride by themselves, astride, not hatless, and wearing more than one type of costume; in fact, one form of dress is worn the first day of the Feria, and we are told that tomorrow they will be wearing another costume and a different form of headdress. The first – for we will take both together, as they are to be seen on later mornings – consists of a leather apron and divided skirt, a white shirt like a man's, a short jacket, and one of the hard-brimmed Córdoban hats. It is a feminine version of what the men are wearing, with the addition perhaps of a rose behind the ear. The thin waist, the level shoulders and hard outline of the hat, worn at a charming angle above a rounded face, such are the attractions of this riding dress, which is infinitely varied in detail and which suits the Spanish type of good looks to perfection.

The other form of costume belongs, as it were, to another tradition; the skirt or trousers, it matters not which, are not so aggressively in imitation of the masculine; the jacket is short, and without the leather apron or leggings is more revealing of the figure; the hair is worn at the back in a snood or chignon, while the hat is a round black one, resembling the crown, without the wings, of the matador's three-cornered

1   Seville: riders at the Feria

2　Avila: the eleventh-century walls

3　Burgos: the late medieval west front of the cathedral

5 Madrid: Hospicio Provincial (1722)

4 Madrid: Puente de Toledo (1723-24)

Both designed by Pedro de Ribera

6 View from Mirador

7 Court of the Lions (1377-91)

8 Granada: The Alhambra. Court of the Lions (begun in 1377)

cap or tricorne. This must, undoubtedly, be its inspiration, and nothing more in the popular tradition of Spain could be imagined than a young woman on horseback in one of these round black hats, or on foot, and wearing, not a snood but a *mantilla de madroños,* which is a scarlet or magenta net with wide meshes worked with bobbles. The soft complexions of the young girls are ravishing to behold, and to compare with the carnation or camellia behind the ear, to which we must add the peculiar beauties of the Spanish horsemanship that allow of so graceful a seat and, where the women riders are concerned, could have been conceived of especially in order to be admired.

But the heat is such that the leather and the painted woodwork feel, by now, like fire. The mules are halted, and after a drink of sherry we drive back to the hotel for luncheon and to take a siesta for the greater part of the afternoon. But at that hour there is nothing else to do in Seville – nothing until about half-past five, when you hear people starting off for the bull fight. Then it is quieter still, and the air is more languorous and somnolent than ever. Perhaps I enjoyed as much as anything else in Seville those hours when the noisier part of the population was at the bull fight. In the shuttered room one's mind filled so easily with nostalgic longings. I would lie there thinking of many things, for another hour or more, until, from all over the town, there would come the sound of castanets, snapping and crackling, hundreds of pairs of them, some fast, some slow; and going to the window I would see the pavements and even the street itself full of a great crowd of persons all converging in this once direction, towards the Feria, a multitude mainly of young women and children, and all playing their castanets as they walk along.

This would be the signal to begin moving towards the coloured fountains and the lights, which go off as we come near to them at the same moment that there is a flicker of lightning and that people standing at the cheap jewellery stalls, close by, look up for rain. But it is better to see the Feria in the sunset – leave it when the lights go on – and come back again. For it is a marvellous sight at this hour. The *casetas* are filling up;

33

dancing has begun, but we will not listen to the music till tonight. We are only aware of it, and of the growing and increasing sparkle upon the air. Instead, we turn down one of the side avenues to the *barracas*, which are the roundabouts and merry-go-rounds of the fair. Here is a stall where they are selling an extraordinary spun concoction, of the consistency of cottonwool, dipping a stick or straw into the frothing, churning mass, drawing it forth with a shock or head of the sugary cottonwool attached, and handing it out as quickly as made, like a sweet cocoon. The sellers of shrimps and *langostinos* are doing a quick trade. There are stalls, too, where coloured drinks, *agraz* or *horchata de chufas*, are sold. But the merry-go-rounds and mountain railways, the miniature motorcars and "witching waves" are no different from those of any other fair. Not so the mountebanks, the like of whom may be extinct in every other country, and who maintain the centuries-old tradition of the actor coming in front of the curtain to advertise the play, with a cracked voice this evening, and through a megaphone. His speech is interminable, and the heat in the crowd such that it is impossible to stand still and listen.

Besides, this is only a few feet away from the open-air restaurants or eating places of the Gitanas. They have established themselves and put up their booths along one entire side of the pavement. The setting is a line of cabins or small *casetas,* a half or a quarter the size of those upon the main avenues, and with chairs and tables arranged in front of them. Unexpectedly, there are white linen cloths upon the tables, but the Gitanas are awarded a prize every year for the cleanest and prettiest arranged of their *casetas*. Even in this noisiest part of the Feria, next to loudspeakers and steam organs, they manage to assert themselves above the din. It has, in fact, spurred them into frenzy.

The younger and more alluring of the Gitanas have come right forward in front of their own tables, into the edges of the crowd, where they stand like bathers in a heavy surf, nearly carried away, and having to struggle in order to get back to the thresholds of their flowering caves or grots. They

34

will come out and pursue you, and be borne along for a little, smiling and cajoling with all the battery of their bright glances, with red lips and fingernails, even and superb white teeth, and smoothed black hair. They are small in height, with the crowns of their heads well below your shoulder, probably no more than fourteen or fifteen years old, and with the rounded faces of their race. In fact, their tawny darkness is extraordinary; and in the background, as if this is not enough, the older women with their snake-like locks – could serpents be as ebony and glossy as a raven's wing – stand in the open doorways, lifting the cauldron lids or stirring, half-hidden in the steam. They have turned this corner of the fair into a nomad encampment, and their unbelievable dark skins at this hour of the evening in the fading light betray the Indian origin of their nation. The old women are in a fury too, and the whole scene of these booths or cabins decorated with flowers and branches is something entirely and absolutely of the Gypsies. There is no other race who have the power to create a nationality and a nomad background by merely cooking something and standing in a door. They have only to do this and it becomes at once the fortune-tellers' tent and the cave of the sorceress.

There is the savour of their world apart in the fumes of their cooking, which has the Oriental pungency and is, at once, an enticement and an alarm. They are frying things in oil and can be seen cooking as though frenzied. Excellent their food is said to be, but not suited to this hot night and to the noise and hubbub. It is to be noticed, moreover, that here they have the entire air of Gypsies, but that they have nearly lost it in their Gypsy suburb of Triana. It must fire their blood to be once more in the smoke and uproar of the encampment. At Roumanian cattle fairs there are these identical open-air restaurants, with roofs of leaves and branches, which are the pleasure gardens of the fair, and that evoke some of the imagery of Rimbaud's *Les Illuminations*. On a particular occasion, upon the plain between Sinaia and Bucharest, they lined both sides of an alley-way, and held some hundreds of persons sitting in the shade, eating their midday meal; the

35

meat was grilling on the charcoal embers, while here and there among the diners musicians wandered, violin in hand, playing popular tunes. There was the same Eastern pungency in the air that I recognized at the Feria, and I now wish more than ever that I had seen the great horse fairs in Moldavia, that last for as long as three days, and had walked late at night by the open-air eating booths. Neither fair, it is true, would allow much time for thinking of the other. Here, in Seville, the cries of the mountebanks, the din of the roundabouts, above all the blare of the steam organs, make the night low-hung and lurid, for all the lights are now switched on, the lines of lamps and lit-up fountains, and we leave the Feria for an hour or two in order to have our dinner.

It was always midnight or after when we returned, a phrase that holds in itself the sensation of the Feria, by which I mean the memory and feeling of the six days it lasted, for it seemed to be a world or experience apart and to go on for ever. At half-past twelve or one o'clock, then, we return by the changing fountains, down the flood-lit avenues, under the festooned arches. A great crowd is still arriving, playing castanets as they walk along, and when we stop in front of the *casetas* there is music coming from nearly every one of them. There are *casetas* belonging to clubs or associations, others that are shared by groups of families, or owned by individuals. They can be of all sizes: as large as a restaurant or quite small; but most are upon the scale of the pierrot's booths upon the sands, with room, that is to say, for a piano and a row of chairs. The chairs are pushed back against the walls, and in the middle is the dancing floor. Many of the *casetas* have had climbing rose trees or flowering creepers trained upon their walls; they have been decorated with posters of bull fights or hung with paintings and family photographs, and furnished, so as to give them the semblance of little rooms. One of the fascinations of the Feria is to pass by such a *caseta* at a moment when an entire family in all its generations – but it may well be two or three families and their friends, one whole side of a little street, or all the inhabitants of some whitewashed court – are resting, exhausted, the older ones sitting staring in front of them, with the smaller children crawling at their feet or asleep upon their knees, awkward upon their chairs as are housewives and small shopkeepers who have to stand all day and, as it were, caught or imprisoned in this cell or interior of their own choice with the enlarged photographs upon the walls and the family piano in the middle of the floor. It is one or two o'clock in the morning, but not one of the smallest children has been put to bed. There is no one left in the house to look after them and they must stay at the Feria till the whole family go home.

Meanwhile the crackle and fire of the castanets is continual and strains of music come from every direction for as far as the lights glitter and the night sky is lit up from the fair. There is this accompaniment of the castanets playing in the crowd as they walk up and down, and the music of the *casetas* as you stand and watch for a moment and move on. There are mechanical pianos which are too loud and drown the music from next door, but at least the music, or nine-tenths of it, is Spanish. There is no "jazz" or "swing". It is, mainly, clapping of hands, and the guitar, *Flamenco* music, good or bad, but on a night like this such is the intoxication from light and sound that the whole body of music becomes lifted and inspired. They are dancing the *sevillana* to an accompaniment of castanets and clicking fingers, to the clapping of hands and the grinding of a guitar, perhaps six or eight young women dancing at once, the older teaching the younger, even little girls of five or six years old in their long-trained crinoline skirts joining in, and one of the younger men of the family standing up, without warning, and taking up the rigid posture of the dance. The *seguidilla* is admired largely for the gracefulness of arms and hands, for the feet do not move much; it is the lascivious grace of the upper part of the body that it is judged by, and by the languorous movements of the wrists. If we would search for an image for the hand and fingers of a dancer in the *seguidilla* it would be that her hands resemble the head of a cobra, or of some other serpent, as it sways its head to hypnotize, and prepares to strike; or that it is like a peacock's head and crest upon that long neck, when the peacock is displaying and makes the snake-like movements of its dance. As a spectacle

37

to watch upon a hot night, and as an expression of the heat, the *seguidilla* is an invention of genius. In which other city of the world or upon what occasion is it possible to watch fifty or a hundred *seguidillas* being danced at one time, and without pause? Only in Seville, and only during the Feria. There is no other population born to this dance, as are the Sevillanas, no other inhabitants who fall naturally into those attitudes or who can wear those flounced dresses so becomingly, being heirs and descendants of the Gaditanian dancers, who "were known" in antiquity "for their agility of body", and Dr. Lemprière, of the *Classical Dictionary,* delighting at the shock, adds, "their incontinency"; but, in fact, the evidence of early Greek travellers points to the inhabitants of Andalucía as running great herds of bulls upon the swamps and plains and to their women as excelling in the dance. The castanets, we are to suppose, come down directly from antiquity, from pre-Roman antiquity, and were borrowed, in all probability, from the temple dancers of the Carthaginians, who, in their turn, had taken them from their ancestors in Tyre and Sidon. This Phoenician heredity or influence is to be seen in so many things that are typically Spanish: in the dance of the Seises before the high altar of Seville cathedral and, contrasting the sacred and profane, in the high combs and mantillas of the Spanish ladies, after the bull fight, as they move about in the American bar of the hotel.

In order the better to appreciate the marvellous spectacle of the Feria it was a good plan to go away from it for half an hour, and so, upon one of the last nights we went to walk in the Barrio de Santa Cruz, a whitewashed labyrinth of narrow alleys lying in a sempiternal moonlight of its own, with doorways, hidden patios, iron well heads, and some of the oldest palaces of Seville. At one end of this there is a garden, touching upon the lovely gardens of the Alcázar, and like those breathing of the orange blossom, and here – it was between one and two o'clock in the morning, in that moonlight begotten of so many whitewashed walls – we heard the sound of voices, and in the tiled space around a fountain found a group of young men and two young women; one unslung his guitar, the others

38

clapped hands rhythmically, there was the crackle of castanets, and the younger of the two girls began to dance the *seguidilla*. This done, they talked excitedly, and she danced again, another form of *seguidilla* with ballet steps, to no tune, only the clapping of hands and the strumming of the guitar. Once again, and yet once more, she danced; a cool air moved among the overhanging branches; the loveliness of this ancient city, the soft and balmy breath of the orange blossom – something I had not known for so many years since the jasmine-laden airs of the Tunisian gardens; airs so pungent and redolent of jasmine that they amounted, almost, to a jasmine civilization, made this scented early hour of the morning, this music, and this dancing into an unbelievably beautiful experience; and all the time, not far away, the night sky was lit with the Feria, and you could hear a continuous, distant roaring, now and then individual voices or strains of music, and the crackling fire and rattle of, perhaps, ten thousand pairs of castanets. It produced an excitement and a beauty that were indescribable. The Feria was beckoning, and we must return.

The *casetas* are numbered. They are referred to by their numbers, and it was to one particular *caseta* that we were on our way, where the dancing was known never to begin till two o'clock in the morning. It belonged to a young lady who bore one of the most famous names in Spain, heiress of one branch of the Borjas or Borgias, and descendant of the Borgia Pope Alexander VI, collaterally related to his bastard Cesare Borgia and to Lucrezia Borgia; a race more proud, now, of San Francisco de Borja and of their descent, on two sides, from the Gothic Kings of León, represented in more modern times by the Duke of Osuna, who was ambassador to the court of the Tsars and was notorious for his extravagance during the years of the Second Empire, and since the extinction of that name living, mostly, upon their Andalucian properties. The Duquesa de Gandía was, in fact, married a year or two ago to a young man of an old family of Seville, and we saw photographs in the newspapers of her wedding procession in a golden coach with footmen and halberdiers wearing the old family liveries. She is herself, we were told, a most graceful and accomplished *Flamenco* dancer, but unfortunately did not dance upon the night we were invited to her *caseta*. With her mother, she was receiving the guests when we arrived, and if we did not see her dance, were able, at least, to agree that she must be. in addition, one of the most beautiful young women in Spain.

Flamenco, in spite of its ever-increasing popularity, is a dying art, comparing in this with Russian Ballet, which became the rage in England, and then in America, just after the last generation of great Russian dancers had ceased to dance. The great period of *Flamenco* music, it is probable, was between 1880 and 1910, at a time, therefore, when no one paid any attention to it, and it flourished in its natural setting of the wineshop and the boarded dancing floor. It is not suited either to the houses of the rich or to the theatre. All the older critics were agreed that *Flamenco* was not what it had been in their youth and that la Niña de los Peines, or her like, had no successors in this generation.

The *caseta* was full of persons and there was, at first, some singing in a high, falsetto voice, after much preluding upon the guitar by a male singer who had been famous, but found it difficult to compete with the strains of a mechanical piano from next door. It was a problem that found its own solution, for after a time the occupants of the next *caseta* fell asleep where they were, or more prosaically went home to bed. Not that the noise and clamour of the Feria were in the least abated. The din was if anything louder than ever, and it was only our good fortune that this particular family or group of friends had tired themselves out upon this third or fourth night of the fair. At one end of the row of chairs, in front, a woman of some sixty years old was sitting, and it was impossible not to be struck by her upright bearing, the carriage of her neck and shoulders, and the confident and alert way that she glanced about her with her extraordinary green eyes. Swarthy skinned, but with something of the air of another Yvette Guilbert and a definite, and marked touch of that period, of the 'nineties and of the drawings and posters of Toulouse-Lautrec, about her. It was whispered to me that this was the famous Pastora

Imperio, who had been the most renowned Gypsy singer of her day; and for a long time we waited on, hoping that she would sing.

She applauded every other singer and showed no inclination to perform, but at last, and without any visible urging, rose to her feet, spoke to the guitarist, and draped her shawl round her, taking care to leave her hands and arms unencumbered. The first chords of the guitar sounded; she seemed to reflect for a moment with closed eyes, the rhythm quickened, she opened her eyes with the alert green fire in them, and her hands and arms became like the hooded cobra or the crested peacock's head while she stamped her feet and achieved the subtle or, alternately, thunderous rhythms that are only to be heard when the Hindu musicians rattle or strike their drums with their fingers or with the palms of their hands. I have never known so strong a proof of the Indian in the Gypsy. She glided forward like the cobra, erect and gliding on its tail, a movement accomplished with an incessant, quick tapping of her feet, her body held quite stiff, clapping or fluttering her palms together, while she leaned her head as though listening to the incantation. She glided in this manner, in succession, to the four corners of the stage, and returning to the centre, stamped her feet in another rhythm altogether, like a roll of drums, and started the long-held, wavering cry of the Gypsy singer. Pastora Imperio is the most controlled singer of *Flamenco* music that I have ever heard; and, as her physical appearance would suggest, she is an artist comparable to Yvette Guilbert, but of the period before that great *diseuse* had forsworn her birthright and turned to little ballads of swains and shepherdesses, to the epoch therefore, as I said, of Toulouse–Lautrec. The great period of *Flamenco* music is present again in all its glory whenever Pastora Imperio is performing, and hers is a mastery which puts all her younger competitors to shame. It is to be imagined upon this evidence what the masters of *Flamenco* must have been before they appeared in drawing-room and music hall. There can be but one or two living singers and dancers of her calibre.

It had been a wonderful sensation to watch this great ex-

41

ponent of the Gypsy art, who must herself, during so many decades, have had such wild, barbaric strains of music running in the head, have seen in her life so much of the stuff of romantic fiction, been married, we were told, to a famous matador, and spent her life in scenes and circumstances so remote from the norm of European or American experience. We could have seen her, ourselves, in no more ideal setting than in this *caseta*, belonging to the last scion of the Borgias. But a still more extraordinary adventure had befallen some persons whom we knew. They had been leaving the Feria very early on the previous morning. It was already light, the sun was rising; and as they walked past the *caseta* they saw that the curtains had been drawn wide and that someone, whom they knew immediately for Pastora Imperio, was dancing in the pale dawn before a small crowd upon the sidewalk who were looking on. Our friends watched this great Gypsy dancer for a few moments, and walked on.

And we must end our account of this marvellous festival of the Feria. There is nothing like it in our contemporary world: no such scene of popular and spontaneous enjoyment. Music as an art of pleasure and excitement plays here, night and day, unspoiled. Beautiful costumes in the Gypsy idiom give sparkle and colour and the illusion of crinolines, but without the whalebone cages. The young women on horseback and their cavaliers form a spectacle without equal as they ride slowly round and round the Feria in the midday heat. To drive among them in a mule carriage while the sidewalks are crowded with Sevillanas in their spotted crinolines is an excitement that is nearly indescribable; then, late in the afternoon, comes that extraordinary moment when from all over Seville, in every direction, you hear the rattle and crackle of castanets. The crowd is making for the Feria and the women are playing their castanets idly, and in anticipation, as they walk along.

Soon they are dancing the *seguidilla* in a hundred different booths at once. All the lights of the fair go on at one and the same time. The fountains change colour. Under the electric lights the crowd is thicker than ever and moves up and down, watching the dancing, to the crackling of its own castanets,

42

which breaks the rhythm; and young girls are dancing in little groups upon the sidewalks. Round midnight the entire Feria is alive with music. Till three o'clock, or after, the dancing is general. It is a marvellous and never-to-be-forgotten feast of sight and sound. As you walk home and look back for the last time, leaving the lights and music behind you, your breath will be caught with the orange blossom, and falling asleep, forgetful of the hour, you may think, as I do, that the Feria of Seville must be the most beautiful public spectacle in the world today.

2. HOLY WEEK

Court of Orange Trees – Las Dueñas – Monuments – Saetas – Processions of Holy Week

It is not to be denied that in Seville, compared with other Spanish towns, we are in a larger sphere, compound, like the Sicilian, from many sources. Palermo is in many respects the only city to compare with Seville. Let us take a look at it. There is in Palermo the same feeling that you may enter an old church and see an Arab or Saracenic ceiling of gilded cedarwood with frieze or cornice of honeycomb or stalactite; or you may bow your head under the drooping daturas, like arum lilies growing downwards, lemon scented, and look upon the five red domes of a little church, an empty ruin, but even in its skeleton it is entirely Eastern. You may pass the fountains of the Quattro Canti, with their Baroque statues of the Seasons, the Spanish Kings, and the Holy Virgins of Palermo; visit the little chapels, the Oratorio della Compagnia del Rosario or that of the Compagnia del Rosario di Santa Zita, so Spanish or even Mexican-sounding, with their stucco decorations by Serpotta, with their benches inlaid with tortoiseshell and mother-of-pearl; or drive out to the Greek temples of Segesta, or to the huge temples hidden in the cornfields at Selinunte.

In Seville, as we say, there is a sense of universality, a feeling of belonging to a larger history. If you cross the Guadal-

43

quivir and go through the Gypsy suburb of Triana, you will reach in a few minutes the ruins of Itálica, a city founded by Scipio Africanus as a home for his veterans of the Carthaginian War, Roman legionaries who had conquered this African colony of the old Phoenicians, laid waste the last great pagan city of the ancient East, overthrown the altars of Moloch, and cut down and burnt the groves of sacred prostitution. Coming back to Seville and entering the Patio de los Naranjos of the cathedral, which is the court of the old mosque, we may walk under the orange trees or look below the arches of the Biblioteca Colombina at the Lagarto (lizard), the stuffed body of a crocodile hanging there under the rafters, and said to have been sent as a present from the Soldan of Great Cairo to Alfonso *El Sabio* in 1260 with a request for his daughter's hand. Or you may look up at the Giralda, the minaret of the old mosque, now the bell tower of the cathedral, and the masterpiece of Jebîr the Moor; which tower has its counterparts by the same Moorish architect at Rabât and at Marrâkesh.

An old palace in Seville such as the beautiful Las Dueñas, belonging to the Duke of Alba, with its patios and fountains, its groves of orange trees and myrtles, is near in plan and conception to a Moorish palace, and though so much older, recalls the tile lined courts and cedar ceilings of the palace of the chieftain El Glaoui at Marrâkesh. The latter building is, indeed, quite modern, and carried out in the old style to its owner's indications, but within view of the snowcapped Atlas mountains that sweep from end to end of the horizon; and knowing both cities, Marrâkesh and Seville, we may feel that the Giralda and the court of orange trees below, the other old palaces such as the Casa de Pilatos of the Dukes of Medinaceli in the Mudéjar style, with its lustre tiles, even the bull fights in the bull ring, might all, just as well, lie below those snowy and mysterious mountains, which would be no more alien to them than is the Sierra Nevada hanging in the sky over Granada.

It is necessary to bear in mind, in the words of a modern historian, that "a considerable portion of the Moslem inhabitants of Spain were of purely Spanish European descent, and this notwithstanding the fact that they were not Christians but Moslems. The fact – that they were in no sense Africans or 'Moors', but heretical Europeans – accounts largely for the bitterness of the European persecution. . . . The Moslems in Spain eventually became just as Spanish as the Christians were. There were Spanish Moslems and Spanish Christians, and what they did and thought belongs equally to the Spanish world. Spain does not mean only Christian Spain."[1] If it did, Trajan, born at Itálica, Seneca and Lucan, both born at Córdoba, and the poet Martial are not Spaniards. But what Christian Spain does account for is the overwhelming power and magnificence of the Church, of which there could be no more thrilling moment of anticipation than now, standing in the court of orange trees and about to enter the cathedral of Seville.

When last I saw it, after the glories of the Feria, an immense wooden structure like a temple painted white and gold, and used for the ceremonies of the Semana Santa, was in process of being taken to pieces near the principal entrance or Puerta Mayor, and nothing could have been better calculated to give scale to the gigantic buildings. This wooden temple is the Monumento, made by an Italian in the middle of the sixteenth century, in which the Host is kept during the night of Thursday in Holy Week and on Good Friday in a silver *custodia* that is one of the masterpieces of Juan de Arfe, in the form of a circular temple of four storeys. The huge wooden pillars, one by one, were being lowered and laid flat upon the ground, a scene of demolition, which made one hear again, in memory or in imagination, the unparalleled ceremonies and processions of the Semana Santa: the Passion and the rending of the white veil (or curtain of the Temple) to the accompaniment of mimic thunder; the washing of the feet; the Miserere of Eslava (that most operatic or lesser or minor composers of church music); the singing of the Gloria when the black veil is torn apart to show the high altar to the peal of thunder and the ringing of the church bells; or the moment

[1] Cf. *The Civilization of Spain*, by J. B. Trend, Oxford University Press, 1944.

45

of the Toque de Gloria, the culmination of all, at midday upon Easter Sunday, when all the bells of Seville sound out together, "when statues of saints are sailing through the streets amid clouds of flowers and glittering candles, and the charivari of voices is broken by the strident, wavering cry of the *saeta,* the impromptu 'arrow of song', of Gitano or *Flamenco* inspiration, uttered by the Gypsies as certain statues pass before them. Their rhapsodic voices, only wrung with penitence and sorrow, speak the sufferings of the Virgin, who is sculptured in her agony weeping and crying. In midst of this the Toque de Gloria, at midday, is indescribable in excitement, a clashing of cymbals as loud as thunder or the roar of cannon."[1]

Long after their echo has died away must some memory of these extraordinary cries stay in the mind. Certain well known *Flamenco* singers are their medium, using that term to the full extent of its meaning, and they are waiting for the processions to come by on the stands erected in the narrow Calle de las Sierpes, or maybe on a balcony. The tall houses to either side and the slow pace of the processions as the *pasos* are borne by make the moment propitious and solemn. Persons who have been again and again to hear the *saetas* and have waited for particular singers to utter their inspiration in these frenzied and rhapsodic cries have described to me this extraordinary moment, which is without parallel in the music of any other land. It is the triumph of the Gypsy genius, the untutored genius of their race that flowers upon the moment in the intoxication of the place and time. The *saeta* may have been in the first place the rhapsodic invention of a single individual, beyond doubt some Gitano, and in its inception it must date from the middle or end of the eighteenth century, when the Spanish idiom in music became established. But at the hands of professional singers during the last half-century its original form of four lines of eight syllables each became enlarged into five or six or more verses, still keeping or even exaggerating the *cante hondo* ornaments and the Moorish influences which are at the back of all Andalucian

[1] Cf. *Sacred and Profane Love,* by Sacheverell Sitwell, 1940, p. 165.

46

music, but magnifying them from the *saeta*, pure and simple, till they took the form of *soleares* or of *seguiriyas*. "Three *saetas* . . . broke from balconies, but were drowned in the rain and tumult of disappointed voices. . . . We could see but could not hear a woman aim a *saeta* at a passing Virgin. . . . Good Friday night we followed the *pasos* to Triana, the Gypsy quarter across the river. The full moon was bright on the river as we caught up with the procession on the bridge. It took a long time to reach the church, for this was the end of the Semana Santa and the *pasos* moved in very short stations, held up by endless *saetas*. Just at the moment of entering the church they burst out again, crowding one upon the other like nightingales in a wood."[1]

Behind the *pasos* walk the hooded penitents of the *cofradías*. It is even a fascination, albeit of a minor order, to see the little figures of *penitentes* in the different colours of the *cofradías* in the windows of the sweetshops – not only in Seville but in Málaga, Murcia, and Granada. For the processions of the Semana Santa are not peculiar to Seville alone. But Seville, Málaga, Granada apart, there is the tendency in the south of Spain at any rate for the ceremonies to vary or alternate from year to year. In the year of writing the grandest ceremonies, perhaps, were those of Cartagena, not a town of any particular interest in itself, though in Cartagena it is impossible to forget that this is the New Carthage of the Phoenicians and Romans, founded by Hasdrubal, the son-in-law of Hamilcar Barca, and the situation and shape of harbour are reminiscent of African Carthage. But Cartagena is not in Andalucía; it lies in the province of Murcia, and we have no wish to forestall our account of that delightful city, which has a Semana Santa with an especial character of its own owing to the sculptured *pasos* of Salzillo. Neither will we anticipate the *penitentes* and the *pasos* of little towns like Orihuela, nor the rivalry of the "Whites" and "Blues" of Lorca.

But we are in the mood to enquire as to the state and origin of the *penitentes*, and for latest information of their strange appearance remove, temporarily, to Málaga, a city where

[1] Miss Beryl de Zoete describing the Semana Santa in *Ballet,* July 1947.

Holy Week is celebrated with a like solemnity, and where a history of the *cofradías malagueñas* has recently been published. From this and other sources it would appear that there are in Málaga no fewer than twenty-seven of the *cofradías*, each with its appropriate symbols and distinctive costume. Each *cofradía* accompanies a pair of groups of sculpture, one portraying a scene from the Passion, and the other a Mater Dolorosa, and each *paso* is carried on the shoulders of some 150 dockers from the port, chosen for their strength. The *pasos* in their embroidered velvet robes at Seville, and before the Civil War at Málaga, are in many instances by Martínez Montañés, Alonso Cano, Pedro de Mena, and other seventeenth-century sculptors of the Andalucian school. The costume of the *penitentes*, it must be explained, is a gown or *túnica*, a long cloak or *capa* reaching to the ground, and a *capirote*, or high, pointed, conical hood covering the entire head and features, with thin slits for the eyes, and covering also the chest and shoulders, while the names of the *cofradías* are taken from the acts or situations of the Passion.

We will look at a few of them as they go by. The *cofradía* of the Coronado (Crown of Thorns), divided like most of the *cofradías* into sections of Christ and of the Virgin, wear a scarlet cloak and white hood or a green cloak and a white hood. The *cofradía* – but we will give its full name, "Fervorosa Hermandad de Ntro. Padre Jesús de la Sentencia y María Santísima del Rosario en sus Misterios Dolorosos" – processes, the one section in violet hood and tunic with white cloak falling to the ground, and the other in *azul* or light blue and white. *Cena* are in white hoods with cloaks in their alternatives of red or *celeste*, which is to say, sky blue. Jesús Cautivo (Christ Captive) – it is curious to read their itinerary through the streets: Comedias (past the theatre), Puente de la Aurora, Cisneros (swans), Alameda (we feel we are following them among the crowds) – appears from head to foot in *capuchón* (monk's robe) of violet with white cloak, or white *capuchón* and cloak of violet.

Humillación are advancing down the Pasillo de Santo Domingo "a las 8 de la noche" past the Puerta del Mar, making the tour of the streets and returning "a su templo" (to the church of Santo Domingo) "a las 2 de la madrugada", dressed in white entirely, hood, cape, and tunic, with the floreated cross of their confraternity in black upon their shoulders, and carrying, perhaps, a light blue banner. *Fusionadas* march by in black gown and bright scarlet hood and cloak. *Expiración*, starting at nine-thirty and returning to their own church at four o'clock in the morning, are more gorgeous still in *tisú de oro* and *terciopelo*, that is to say, in hoods of cloth-of-gold and cloaks of blue velvet, or alternatively in hoods of cloth-of-silver and immense black cloaks. And we identify *Sangre* in scarlet with white cloaks; *Amargura* in white gowns and violet or crimson damask; *Soledad* all in blue; and *Sepulcro*, terrifying, in black from head to foot.

The town, Málaga or Seville, it matters not which, seems to be entirely taken over and administered during Holy Week by these hooded Inquisitors. They are to be seen, when not in procession, walking to their duties. The towering height of their hoods and the entire anonymity of their features hidden under their cowls impart to them a collective individuality due to their groups of colours, so that the resemblance is more to families of birds than to human beings. We know their archetype, by instinct, from the cowled and hooded figures of the Holy Inquisition, and we are arrived, here, in the metropolis of the hood and cowl. We begin to apprehend certain attitudes of this race of hooded men and it is not long before we know the fixed poses of their heads and hands: those who walk together in pairs, without the *capa* or wide cloak, and holding a staff or a wax candle in their hand; those in black or in sky blue, without cloaks, too, and holding great lanterns or holy banners; or the cloaked ones, talking together, inclining their masked heads, and whether their cloaks are white, purple, blue, or scarlet. *Cena*, in white hoods and gowns and scarlet or pale blue cloaks, contrast magnificently with *Huerto*, who stand about in white gowns and cloaks and hoods of violet or sky blue. And there are the scarlet of *Calvario* and the full crimson or purple-violet of *Amargura*. There are to be seen, in all, some forty different variations of these colourings.

Nothing like this procession or invasion of a great city by these hooded, masked penitents can have had existence in ordinary experience. The hooded costume of the *cofradías* must date from the fifteenth century, at latest, for their cloaks and thin, high, tapering hoods could be nothing other than medieval in inspiration,[1] and for a parallel we have to turn to Italian drawings and engravings of the life of Pulcinella, that show a world inhabited by Pulcinellas who are engaged in all the ordinary activities of daily life. By the same token we return from Málaga to Seville. All the images, as we have seen, are carried down the Calle de las Sierpes to the Town Hall, where they are greeted by the Alcalde (Lord Mayor), and thence through the cathedral and back to their parish churches after a march which has lasted from ten to twelve hours.

We hear again the trumpet and the drum. The images are being borne along the narrow streets, or *calles*. And with the trumpet and the drum coming nearer, step by step, or dying away into the distance, we admire the velvet robes of the Virgins, "of crimson, apple-green, ivory, or eau-de-nil", covered or netted with a mesh of embroidery in gold and silver thread, mantles which are still being made and that represent a living art of embroidery parallel to that devolving around the *capote de paseo* of the matador, with its roses and carnations in brilliant colours.

The Jesús del Gran Poder is approaching or has been carried through the great cathedral. Such is the destiny of all the *pasos*, this once a year. One, the Virgen del Gran Dolor, "has a jewelled dagger thrust into her breast, and the tears on her smooth, pure cheeks are real pearls". Or it is the turn of la Virgen de la Esperanza, la Macarena, the beloved idol of the poor, who still bears on her left cheek the scar from the wine glass which was thrown at her by a man in drunken ecstasy, a crime which he expiated by walking in chains for eight years in succession among the hooden *penitentes*. We see

[1] The black-hooded brothers of the Misericordia are to be seen in the streets of Florence. Their oratory, a medieval building, stands in the Piazza del Duomo.

50

the veils of the Virgins, their inclined heads, and starry crowns. They are under golden canopies, and their long trains reach out behind them nearly to the gound. And the *pasos* are heaped high with flowers. They come by in breaths of roses and carnation, in self-engendered gales of jasmine and of orange blossom – and in a blaze of candles.

And now, with the tumultuous sound of all the processions from the different parishes in our ears as they carry round their idols, with the trumpet and the drum sounding in every direction, and the agonized sculptures in their jewelled and embroidered robes being carried past, we are in the mood to enter the vast cathedral and find it empty, for the entire population are upon the streets or on their balconies. Seville cathedral is the largest Gothic church in Christendom and the cathedral that is most typical of Spain. Almost certainly – and this is typical, too – the work of unknown French architects in the beginning, but taking on Spanish character, we might say, from the moment that the design was settled. It is by no means one of the most beautiful of Gothic churches, but it impresses by sheer size, and then overwhelms with the riches of its treasury, due to the gold and silver of Mexico and Peru, and with the solid magnificence of its Spanish ironwork, the *rejas*, or grilles, or the Capilla Mayor in particular being of impressive height and the work of the great ironsmith Fray Francisco de Salamanca. Nothing of its sort in Spain exceeds the splendour of the golden *retablo*, by the Fleming Maestre Dancart and other sculptors, and it is a wonderful sensation to stand on the high altar steps at the foot of it, but a few inches away, and to look up at the incredible profusion or flowering of gilt figures, an experience that will never be forgotten if the cathedral organist, a Basque, happens at the time to be playing a Bach fugue.

There are sculptures by Montañés; there are paintings by Murillo. In the Sacristía Mayor and the Sala Capitular there are jewels and plate and vestments of intrinsic value but not of great importance as works of art. There is, in short, everything that there should be in the biggest and most splendid cathedral in all Spain. But the sculpture of Montañés is better ap-

51

preciated when the *pasos* are borne by; Murillo is seen to more advantage in his paintings at the Hospital de la Caridad, which were much admired a hundred years ago (but taste changes!); where may be seen, as well, four paintings by Valdés Leal, a painter who loved the charnel house, together with the portrait and the sword and death mask of Don Miguel de Mañara, wrongly associated with Don Juan Tenorio (Don Juan or Don Giovanni). There are excellent paintings by Zurbarán in the Museo Provincial, especially the white monks in their refectory, brought from the Cartuja, and the single figures of St. Bonaventura and other fashionably attired virgins. Beautiful and touching in sentiment are the convent churches in the old quarter of the town, with their tiled walls and Mudéjar ceilings, San Clemente, Santa Clara, Santa Paula, the first named of which is so gentle in poetry that for a few days after I first saw it, more than twenty years ago, I could think of nothing else and can only fix or recapture for a little space this other moment in time when I recall that I was told of one of the nuns who had gone from the convent to join another house of her order in Mexico, and who wrote back to her relations that no one in Mexico talked or thought of anything by Manolete.

In the court of this convent, on the evening I saw it again, the old people were sitting under the orange trees talking or working at their embroidery; you could hear the droning of the nuns in their choir, like the sound of summer bees high up in the honeycombs of the *artesonado* ceiling; and in the far corner a young girl, little more than a child, was practising the *seguidilla*. From all over Seville came the distant murmur of castanets. It was another evening of the Feria. It must have been this world and this mode of life that the young Disraeli, a Spanish Jew, had in mind over a hundred years ago when he wrote home in a letter[1]: "Few Spanish families retire till two. A solitary bachelor like myself still wanders, or still lounges on a bench in the *warm* moonlight. The last guitar dies away... you, too, seek your couch, and amid a gentle, sweet

[1] Disraeli was descended from the New Christian houses of Aboab, Cardoso, and Villareal, cf. *A History of the Marranos*, by Cecil Roth, Philadelphia, 1941, p. 318.

flow of loveliness, and light, and music, and fresh air, thus dies a day in Spain."

3. ROMERIA

Granada – The Alhambra – Tombs of Ferdinand and Isabella – The Cartuja – Albaicín – Generalife – Córdoba – Ronda – Jerez – Romería del Rocío

The Semana Santa, the Feria, and the Romería, these are the types of religious festival in Andalucía, and we propose to include some account of a Romería. The Spanish dictionary gives "pilgrimage, picnic, excursion" as the meaning of the word, and this is exact as an interpretation. A Romería is a country festival that involves a journey, often of elaborate length and duration. The Romerías may draw the population of a whole province. They are not to be compared, therefore to those other beautiful occasions of the same kind, the pilgrimages in Moravia and Slovakia that are held upon saints' days, when wonderful peasant costumes are to be seen, but the affair is entirely local and confined to a radius of a few miles. More than anything else the Romerías are an expression of the aptitude for enjoyment of the Andalusians. This is their prime quality, and to its fulfilment they bring their innate artistic feeling. In a climate like that of the south of Spain it is profitless to be for ever searching for a serious purpose – whether it be behind a religious ceremony or a building. Often enough the message is no more than an expression of gaiety and high spirits. The Spaniards themselves, it is probable, have never lost sight of this, but it is a secret that has long been forgotten among the Anglo-Saxons.

It is a fact that the "hard" school of Victorian ecclesiologists, headed by those architects who returned home to erect town halls and railway stations in the Gothic style, has contrived to divert attention for nearly a century from the beauties of Andalucía and the south of Spain. The southern buildings, their conscience warned them, were effeminate and sugary compared to the manly Gothic of the north, and it is possible,

53

even now, to meet persons who confess themselves shocked by the Alhambra. Readers of Street's *Gothic Architecture in Spain* will remember how he avoided Andalucía; but he belonged to a generation which had undergone a surfeit of the picturesque, and it was precisely for the reason that Seville and Granada were so easy to like that he felt drawn towards the sterner buildings of the north.

The indiscriminating enthusiasm of what we would term the theatrical view of Spain is amusingly illustrated in one of the volumes of the "Landscape Annual" (for 1837) which contains a steel engraving after David Roberts of the Hospicio Provincial at Madrid. This doorway by Pedro Ribera, architect of the Puente de Toledo (at Madrid), is one of the wildest fantasies of the followers of Churriguera, and it is safe to say that from that day till recent times no one has had the temerity to admire it. But to David Roberts the Hospicio Provincial was picturesque – and picturesque it is! David Roberts, we note, having received his early training with a travelling company at Carlisle, obtaining more regular employment at the Theatre Royal, Edinburgh, and working after that for Drury Lane and Covent Garden. The Spain of David Roberts, it is evident from this, could not be the Spain of G. E. Street. But it is Spain, nevertheless, and an aspect of Spain that now, after a century, is regaining favour. And that, despised or unnoticed, was there all the time, more particularly in the sunny climate of Andalucía and the Levante. More things than a mere change of morale are implicit in this altered or extended view. We may imagine for ourselves, if we like to do so, how much a minor artist like David Roberts, with his stage training, would have made of Mexico, and how little appeal it would have had to the school of Ruskin.

This contempt for an architecture of fantasy does not exist among the Spaniards for whom the Baroque, like the Plateresque, has all the force and beauty of a particular school of poetry, and who love the south for its climate and its orange groves. They are the inheritors of the soil: but if I tell the following anecdote it is in order to prove what are the feelings for Andalucía of those followers of another religion whom they dispossessed. When I was in Marrâkesh and some of my family wished to see the interior of a harem, we were led by our guide to the door of a palace where the Caid, an old Moor with a white beard, was sitting in the sun."Tell him," said the guide, "that you have come from Seville and Granada and he will be so interested that he will not notice and they can walk inside." The plan worked admirably. We conversed in halting French; and they had returned from seeing the harem and talking to one of his wives, the daughter of a Sultan, before he had half-done with his questions about "ce que nous Maures appelons la terre promise".

Andalucía has, decidedly, many of the concomitants of a promised land. How must the Berbers have found it coming out of the wastes of Africa! But the traveller is almost to be pitied who sees Morocco first, and then Granada. It is, indeed, almost impossible, looking down over that city from the Alhambra, not to listen for the sounds and voices of an Oriental town. And it is curiously dead: dead, above all, compared not to an Eastern town but to the astonishing charivari of voices and of noises of every description that you hear if you look down over Naples from the balcony of the Belvedere in the Certosa di San Martino high above that town. The only sounds at the Alhambra come from the opposite hill of the Albaicín. But to be standing on the Alhambra hill, already, is to forestall any description of the approach to Granada, which must always be thrilling because of the first view of the huge red adobe castle covering the hill above the deep gorge of the Darro, with the snowy Sierra in the background.

The "effeminacy" of the Alhambra is confined to the interior. The exterior, with its red walls and towers, is proud and masculine to a degree, although the Torre de la Cautiva and the Torre de las Infantas at the far end of the hill, a long way from the main body of the Alhambra, contain some of the most delicate work of the Moors in stalactite and filigree. The Alhambra is one of the supremely beautiful sites in the world, and it is as difficult to find anything new to say about it, as it would be to describe, once and for all, the Acropolis or the Taj Mahal. The Hall of the Ambassadors, leading from

55

the Court of the Myrtles, has the most beautiful and breath-taking of views, for its foundations are carried right forward so that you look out from the *mirador* over the town below. It has, also, a superb cedarwood domed ceiling with a pattern of hundreds of polygons and intersecting lines. The Court of the Lions is so famous and so fantastically lovely that perhaps it may be said that the Maghribian or Moroccan fantasy here surpassed itself and verges on the Indian. But it has been re-marked before that the twelve stone lions carrying the basin of the fountain are related in style to the lions that support tombs and pulpits in Calabria and Apulia. The fountain itself, there-fore, might be Norman-Saracenic. Nothing could be more fanciful than the filigree pavilions at either end. The two halls at opposite sides of the court, the Hall of the Abencer-rages and the Hall of the Two Sisters, we would describe as veritable triumphs of the apiarist, and the bees have, indeed, formed their honeycombs in the angles of the ceiling. Such is the effect of the *media naranja* and stalactite decoration of the Moors. In the Hall of the Abencerrages the ceiling rises from eight stalactite pendentives to a sixteen-sided cupola lit by as many little windows. The Hall of the Two Sisters offers the most extraordinary agglomeration of the honeycells, which cling to one another, and drip down, surge up into another cluster, and change the square of the room into an octagon, a polygon, with a fantasy and an elaboration that it is not pos-sible to describe in words. The arched entrances to this pair of halls are fringed with stalactites, and apart from the view down over Granada from the *mirador*, the most beautiful sensation of the whole Alhambra is to look from one to the other across the Court of the Lions, because the stalactitic arches are at different levels and there is a moment when you see all four of their arabesqued outlines one against the other, which is the intended climax of this Oriental poetry.

Why is it that the Alhambra, with so many beauties, is a little boring; that the first sight of its interior is better than the second or the tenth; and that, in the end, the red walls and towers become more beautiful than the memory of those honeycombs and stalactites? Not only that, but there comes

a time when sooner than stand again in the Hall of the Abencerrages or the Hall of the Two Sisters, we find ourselves
admiring the unfinished Palace of Charles V nearby, its Renaissance façade in white stone, and the circular court of two
storeys by Pedro Machuca – a court intended for tournaments
and bull fights, but its Italian speech in units or syllables of
the Doric and Ionic may remind us of Caprarola by the great
Vignola, of the Villa Farnesina in Rome, itself, and of the
classical poetry which no Moor, no Moslem has ever under-
stood.

Even so, after the Alhambra it is an anti-climax to come
down the hill. The cathedral of Granada is by Enrique de
Egas, architect of the Hospital Real at Compostela and of the
Hospital de Santa Cruz at Toledo. "Los Reyes Católicos",
Ferdinand and Isabella, the conquerors of Granada and heirs
of the New World, lie buried in the Capilla Real in white marble
tombs by a Florentine, Domenico Fancelli, but the tombs and
the chapel itself are less impressive than the Capilla del Condestable at Burgos, with its eight-pointed star-vault; than the
chapel of Miraflores; or those of Santiago or of los Reys Nuevos at Toledo. More interesting is the triptych by the Fleming,
Dirck Bouts; or the pair of organ cases, with their salvos and
fusillades of pipes. When I was in Granada some years ago
I saw the curious ceremony of the appointment of a new
archbishop. Two young men had arrived at our hotel rather
noisily, the previous evening, and we were told they came from
Rome. Early next morning we were in our places in the cathedral; the great doors of the nave were locked and barred; there
was the sound of loud knocking, the doors were flung open
and the two young men, now booted and spurred, wearing the
white buckskin breeches, the breastplates, and plumed helms
of the Pope's Guardia Nobile, strode up the entire length of
Granada cathedral, from the west door to the high altar, where
they halted, and one of them read out a long declaration of
appointment, in Latin, from a scroll of vellum.

The kneeling figures of the Gran Capitán Gonzalo de Córdoba, conqueror of Naples, and of his wife are to be seen in
the desecrated church of San Gerónimo, now a cavalry bar-

racks, a work of Diego de Silóee, architect of the Escalera Dorada in Burgos cathedral. And somewhere in this vicinity was one of the most extraordinary of all Spanish buildings, the Castillo de Bibataubin, which perished in the Civil War. The Castillo de Bibataubin was a barracks. It had a long façade with a tower at either end, the whole painted red like a soldier's tunic, but with white ornaments like the soldier's pipeclay. At the corners of the towers, high up on the walls, there stood statues of grenadiers wearing the tall, half-sugar-loaf hats of the Prussian Guard in the wars of Frederick the Great. They had powdered hair tied down into a pigtail, bristling moustachios, and muskets on their shoulders. In the centre of the façade was a doorway flanked by a pair of twisted or Salomonic pillars, another pair of *salomónicas* above, to each side of a balcony guarded again by grenadiers in niches, while over the balcony sat a lion on a stone cushion, brandishing a drawn sword and wearing a crown.

This most peculiar of barracks was a distorted echo of the parade grounds of Potsdam, here in Granada, under the Alhambra walls. One wonders what was its inspiration? The date of the Castillo de Bibataubin was 1752–1764, and it was at about this time that the music of the Marcia Real was sent, according to tradition, by Frederick the Great to Ferdinand VI of Spain with the advice that it should be played upon twelve silver flutes. The Marcha Real, which used to be played in the forecourt of the Royal Palace at Madrid for the changing of the guard, is a grenadier march. It may have been composed by Frederick himself, but is more probably by Johann-Joachim Quantz, the giant Prussian who taught Frederick to play the flute, was constantly in attendance upon him, and composed a total of six hundred concertos and other pieces for his favourite instrument. Ferdinand VI, for his part, was patron of Farinelli, the greatest of the *castrati*, whom he had inherited from his father, Philip V, the first of the Bourbon kings of Spain. The Infanta Barbara of Portugal, wife of Ferdinand VI had Domenico Scarlatti for her private composer and was herself a considerable performer upon the harpsichord. This pair of royal melomaniacs had, presumably, been in correspondence with the King of Prussia and had sent a request for some of his music, and we may think we catch in the Castillo de Bibataubin some distant echo of their curious reign.

But in Granada there is another most fantastic building. This consists in additions made to the Cartuja in the eighteenth century, and it comprises the Sagrario and the Sacristía. The Sagrario is of marble, porphyry, and jasper, and its faceted and fluttering pilasters prepare us for the Sacristía. Designed by Hurtado in 1713, this hall was not begun until 1730 by Luis de Arevalo, a stonemason, with the assistance of a stuccoist Luis Cabello, and it was not completed until some time between 1771 and 1783. The doors and presses of cedarwood inlaid with ebony, mother-of-pearl, tortoiseshell, and silver are the work of a Carthusian monk, Fray José Manuel Vásquez, from 1730 to 1764. The Sacristía is of an intense, snowy whiteness, formed from innumerable white edges fluttering and never touching, but the stucco is relieved from monotony by the pilasters of red marble with white and pink veins and by the tortoiseshell of the presses.

Théophile Gautier was the first to appreciate the Cartuja and to realize the aim of this pair of halls, which was to rival the stucco arabesques of the Alhambra. They are in a style of their own, which appears nowhere else in Europe, and in terms of ornament their only equivalents lie in Mexico: in the doorway to the Santuario de Ocotlan, at Tlaxcala, an affair of identical white fluttering pilasters and edges under an immense recessed hood or shell. The towers at Ocotlan, to either side, are of lozenge-shaped vermilion bricks set in white stucco, giving an effect as of scarlet shagreen, while their upper storeys are dazzlingly white, with fretted cornices and Salomonic pillars. This whole exterior could be the work of Luis de Arévalo. A pure-blooded Indian, Francisco Miguel, worked for twenty-five years on the interior, converting it into a kind of golden grotto; while another Mexican church, the Seminario de San Martín, at Tepozotlan, has a *camarín*, or hall, in which the vestments for the image of the Virgin are kept, that could without exaggeration be said to belong to

59

the Granadine interpretation of the school of Churriguera, but in gold, scarlet, blue, light and dark green, and silver — of metallic lustre, not of snowy whiteness.

Francisco Hurtado Izquierdo was born at Lucena in 1669 and died in Priego in 1728. Mr. R. C. Taylor sees him influenced by the Capella del Crocifisso in the cathedral at Monreale, above Palermo, dated 1692, an affair of inlaid marbles and Salamonic columns by Giovanni da Monreale. I am unable to agree with him. On the other hand, I have never seen Hurtado's other chief work, beside the Cartuja of Granada, the Sagrario of the Cartuja of El Paular, in the pinewoods above Segovia.[1] But Mr Taylor, and this is most interesting, traces his influence in two emigrant architects to Mexico, Jerónimo Balbao of Cádiz, who built the altar of the Kings in the Cathedral of Mexico City; and more exciting still, in Lorenzo Rodríguez, an architect from Guadix, who built the Sagrario Metropolitano, a parish church built on to the cathedral, and one of the finest specimens of the Churrigueresque in all Mexico (1749). It is in the plan of a Greek cross with, not one, but two intricate façades of white stone, connected by a wall of pink or red *tezontle*. The Churrigueresque altars are all gone. Rodríguez built another church, La Santísima, in Mexico City, a façade of three storeys, with pilasters, inverted pyramids, and side walls of red *tezontle*. It has a tower capped with the triple crown of the Papacy. Here, too, the interior has been gutted. But Rodríguez left Guadix before the choir stalls were made, and Mr Taylor ascribes them to F. X. Pedraxas, the "last epigone of the school of Hurtado". To Pedraxas he ascribes, also, the Sagrario of the parish church at Lucena: ". . . the masterpieces of Pedraxas are all in Priego. His greatest work is undoubtedly the Sagrario at Priego, without a shadow of doubt one of the greatest works in the whole history of the Rococo . . . there are better things in Priego

---

[1] Other works by Hurbado include the Sacristía of Cardinal Salazar in the cathedral of Córdoba, the cardinal's tomb, and the Hospital of the destitute in the same city. In Granada he designed the Sagrario of the cathedral, the altar of St. James, and the marble pulpits, and the Camarin of N.S. de las Angustias.

than in the whole of Valencia, the Palacio de Dos Aguas included". I thank Mr. Taylor for this information; never having heard word, before, of the fine buildings at Priego, which must be as interesting as Lecce or as Noto. But there is always something new in Spain.

So far have we travelled from Granada. But it is only in order to return and climb the steep hill of the Albaicín. Here, among the cactuses and prickly pears, are the luxury dwellings of the troglodytes and, indeed, of all Spanish cave dwellers, a considerable population, beginning with some whom we saw sunning themselves on that first evening of spring, sitting at the doors of their caves in the yellow sunset, as we came down through Aranda de Duero upon the road to Madrid; and continuing with the villages of troglodytes just before we reached La Bañeza. Both the outsides and interiors of the caves are whitewashed upon the Albaicín, and the daughters of the Gypsies come pouring down the hillside in their bright-coloured skirts as out of the tunnels of a rabbit warren, running and jumping with the long-straddled stride of their race, past the laundry put out to dry upon the cactus hedges. They have castanets in their hands, a guitar is brought from nowhere, and they begin to dance. Some of the young girls of the Albaicín are remarkably pretty in the dark Gypsy manner, but they wear lipstick and have varnished nails and the whole performance is too obviously put on for tourists. This is no true academy of Gypsy dancing.

And, yet, the Albaicín is an integral part of one of the beautiful places in the world. The Gypsies have been settled here for four hundred years. The lower slopes of the hill had, before that, been the refuge of Moors from Baeza. Here, too, they congregated after the fall of Granada, and were massacred, and the Moorish quarter burnt down during the revolt of the Moriscos in 1569. So the Gypsies settled in the ruins of the Moors, and indeed something of the kind may be seen in the outskirts of all cities in Morocco where there are Bedouins living in the ruins. It is impossible at Granada not to be reminded at every turn of Meknes or Fez. But Granada has not the deep melancholy of the Moorish towns; nor the fevered sights and noises of the *souks*. And the greatest beauty of Granada we have kept for the last word. It must be, indeed, one of the supreme beauties of the whole world. If all other memory of Spain were dead and gone and there was to be nothing else left to indicate what meanings and implications are attached to the "Spanish" adjective in every language, then the gardens of the Generalife would be one of the objects that must be saved. Two others could be *Las Menias* of Velázquez and almost any piece of Spanish music!

The gardens of the Generalife, in their origin, were the summer villa of the Moorish kings and date from the first quarter of the fourteenth century. Their history is one of complication, for after the fall of the city they came into possession of Don Pedro de Granada, a descendant of the old Moorish kings of Almería and a Moorish renegade, through whom they devolved, down the centuries, upon the Grimaldi Pallavicini family of Genoa, who became marquises of Campotéjar.

Years ago the gardens were wonderfully and beautifully neglected. No member of the family had come from Italy for many years to visit them. Now they have been bought by the Spanish state and are kept up with just the right degree of attention, the guardians, unlike those at the Alhambra, who spoil its beauty with their importunities, being unobtrusive but always at hand, if wanted, to answer any question or enquiry. New avenues of cypresses have been planted, and the flowerbeds are lovely with blue and white irises and Spanish roses.

The entrance to the Generalife is down a long and curving lane of cypress, warm with that resinous and furry scent. This leads into a larger and straight avenue heightening our expectancy. Down below there is the flower garden seen through the green stems. Then the Moorish arches and the *mirador* over them appear at the far end of a long, thin canal with jets of water throwing up and forming arches of spray down its whole length, between hedges of clipped cypress and two long rows of buildings. This is the court of the Generalife, and although renewed at different periods, it must be the most ancient example of a Moorish garden. The sound of waters is as melodious as at Villa Lante. And there are cascades, as at Villa Lante or Capraròla, but of Moorish origin, running down the balustrades of a stone stairway, and an upper garden and grottos that are noisy and humid with the falling waters. The loggia – for it would be called that in Italy – has one of the inlaid Moorish ceilings, and there are arabesques upon the walls; but all is simplicity. It is fountains, cypresses, and arches; for the lovely flower garden is an improvement of our own times. And the view? It is impossible to think of anything more physically beautiful than the view down over Granada and on to the red walls and towers of the Alhambra. For the Generalife projects far forward above the valley and stands higher than the Alhambra. It looks down over the ravine of the Darro to the Albaicín. In all but its lack of sculpture the Generalife could be an Italian garden. It has the line of beauty of Villa d'Este, of Caprarola, of Villa Lante, of the great gardens of the Italian Renaissance which were the works of Vignòla and of Pirro Ligorio. But, being of the Orient, it has no sculpture. And this simplicity betrays its age and gives it further beauty. The Generalife will for ever have an association with the composer Falla who so loved it. And, indeed, it is nearer to music than to any of the other arts. Or so it would seem, looking down over the Alhambra and hearing the tumbling waters and the nightingales.

Just as Villa d'Este looks down from Tivoli over the *campagna*, so does the Generalife give upon the *vega* of Granada. It is like a kind of fiery intoxication to drive through this country in the golden sunset, for it is within view of the snowy *sierra*, but of an African richness sporting the palm tree and the sugar cane. Out in the middle of this tropical fertility, but in a landscape of tossing and painted hillocks, lies the town of Guadix, famous for the Barrio de Santiago, a suburb of Gypsies living in caves scooped out of the soft clay, and whitewashed. And it would be tempting to set forth from Granada to the port of Motril, on the Mediterranean, in a landscape "like that of the Antilles", in midst of date palms and sugar canes, stopping on the way at Ujijar in order to look for the "half-Moorish race" of Ford, and for the "women with apricot cheeks and black eyes and hair, who gaze wildly at the stranger from little porthole windows, scarcely larger than their heads".

Andalucía is not to be thought of in terms of one temperament, for it differs widely in its various parts. The "African-looking" types of Almería and its district are far removed from those of Córdoba, a town of which Manolete, the idol of Spain, lately killed in the bull ring, was a typical inhabitant. According to Spaniards, the sombre, cold gravity of his technique put him apart from the more showy, theatrical school of Seville. With Manolete display and gesture were at a minimum. His lean, thin figure was of another air and water from the city that gave birth to Figaro. And indeed Córdoba, lying coldly on its hillside and first caught sight of nearly twenty miles before you come to it by road resembles some Eastern city. Seen from far away, it has reminded me of Mostar (in Herzogovina), until I half expected to meet hooded and veiled women in its streets, for it is visible for about the same distance out of the rocky hills and there is the same sensation of surprise at finding a large and ancient city in so bare and inhospitable a landscape.

Córdoba, like so many Oriental towns from Anatolia to North Africa, is entered by a Roman bridge, but it is surprising to look up from that to the Triunfo, a column with gilded statue in honour of the Archangel Raphael by a pair of Provençals, Graveton and Verdiguier, trying hard, and unsuccessfully, to be Rococo. There is no other architecture in the world like the Mezquita, the most Moorish of buildings, but not at all Moroccan, for this is no specimen of the Maghribian style. Its forest of columns, and double or intersecting arches of red brick, alternating with white stone, are in the earlier or Syrian manner, for the mosque is of the ninth century, coeval with those of Cairo and of Kairouan. This is the more understandable because 'Abd-ar-Rahmân, who founded the Emirate of Córdoba, was an Omayyad, fled from the massacre of his family at Damascus. The Mezquita is one of the most interesting but not most beautiful buildings in the world, much as we may admire the mathematical ingenuity of the Moorish vaulting; and lost in the middle of it lies the Capilla Mayor, which we venture to think is not so inappropriate as harsh criticism would have us believe. Were the mosque restored to its original bareness it would need its prostrated worshippers and prayer mats, and the Patio de los Naranjos its fountains for ablutions. But the *coro* is of a dusty magnificence profiting, even, from lack of admiration. The great Spanish organ cases (whence years ago I heard magnificent playing of a Bach fugue), the huge open choir books on their stands, the brass balustrades are splendid. The *sillería,* seating over a hundred, is Churrigueresque of the middle of the eighteenth century from the hand of the sculptor Pedro Duque Cornejo (1677–1757); while the Frenchman Verdiguier, now with an added "Miguel" to his name, carved the giant pulpits resting on the symbols of the four evangelists. What we would regret in Córdoba, since the mosque can never again be restored to the Moslems, are the Córdoban ivory caskets, the most beautiful of their kind (there is one in the Victoria and Albert Museum, another in the cathedral at Pamplona and one more at Braga in Portugal), and the silken stuffs; the *dibaj* (of many colours), the *tiraj* with names of Caliphs and Emirs worked upon them; the thousand looms of the Kingdom for weaving the stuffs called *Iskalaton* (scarlet), the like number for robes called *Al Jorjani* (Georgian), the like for robes called *Isbahani* (from Isfahan), or the manufactury of turbans of gay and dazzling colours for the Moorish women. It is poor consolation to go, instead, into the church of El Carmen for its pictures by Valdés Leal, even though this necrophilic painter did the engravings for an old book, La Torre Farfán, *Las Fiestas de Sevilla,* 1672.

It is not possible to dwell upon Andalucía for many moments together without returning to the popular festivals. With the sounds of that phrase *las fiestas de Sevilla* ringing in our ears we have a vision of the spangled dresses of the *toreros,* which became fixed in time in the last decades of the eighteenth century, in the epoch, precisely, of the tapestries of Goya, when the rules of the bull fight were drawn up by the famous Pedro Romero, not in the bull ring of Seville, but in

65

that of Ronda. The costume, therefore, may owe as much to Ronda as to Seville, and must be influenced by the old smuggler-mountaineer character of the Rondeños, but in a stage or circus version of that, as behold the spangles! Ronda has a bull ring of the time, built late in the eighteenth century by the Real Maestranza, the oldest of the equestrian corporations in all Spain. It has wrought iron balconies with tauromachic scenes, and is to be considered the *locus classicus* of the bull fight. The cold mountain air of Ronda and the purity of its conditions, away from the population of a big town, may have affected the restraint of the Rondeño school, but that the *torero* dresses of Pedro Romero and his pupils and contemporaries were of a high fantasy may be seen in the statuettes of bull fighters belonging to a famous collection in Seville.[1] There are eight or ten wax figures dressed in actual stuffs; they are attributed to Goya himself and it is not improbable that he had some hand in their designing. Pedro Romero appears in a long stocking cap reaching to his waist; and there are coats and breeches of such vivid colours that the bright red harlequin *torero* in cocked hat and with yellow and light-blue patterning or embroidery upon him, the most daring of Picasso's Andalucian inventions for *Le Tricorne,* is no exaggeration. It is of such figures that we must think, coming away from the Plaza de Toros in Ronda and passing a wrought iron window grille which is one of the chief beauties of the town, a kind of fanciful metal birdcage through the bars of which the women could carry on whispered conversations with their gallants. This window grille dates from the late seventeenth century and is among the most elaborate in Spain. But Ronda is one of the most beautiful of hill towns, with its gorge and tremendous bridge and with eagles for ever soaring below the level of its cliffs.

Cádiz I have never liked, although there is a fascination in the approach to it through San Fernando and along the narrow isthmus, because of the one-storeyed whitewashed houses with "jalousies" outside their windows throwing blue shadows on the walls, and because of the *salinas*, or salt marshes, where

[1] The Duque del Infantado.

flocks of white ibis may be seen and in the distance there are white pyramids and stacks of salt, "glistening", in Ford's fine phrase, "like the white ghosts of the British tents when our redjackets were quartered here", in the wars of Wellington. There are Murillos in Santa Catalina, if you run the gauntlet down the corridors of a large lunatic asylum, while the museum has some of Zurbarán's Carthusian paintings from the Cartuja de Jerez. But of all traditions of music and venery, its cuisine and dancing girls, the *jocosae Gades* of Juvenal and Martial, the *improbae Gaditanae,* nothing is left. Cádiz is the city where Manuel de Falla was born, and it was the canons of the cathedral who commissioned Haydn to compose "The Seven Last Words from the Cross". Such are the last contributions of Cádiz to the dwindling aesthetic pleasures.

Jerez de la Frontera, on the other hand, is one of the pleasantest and most prosperous towns in Spain, owing to its vineyards, less picturesque now than formerly, when there were storks nesting on the church towers and the Churrigueresque Colegiata and the late Gothic San Miguel had an added beauty from neglect and decay. But the Cartuja, outside the town, is the lion of Jerez, with a façade of golden stone in "Apulian" style, pertaining to the school of Lecce, in two storeys of eight pillars each, with the sharp carving of San Cataldo or the Seminario of that Southern Italian town, a Gothic interior, and enormous and deserted cloisters. This convent was once famous for its Zurbaráns. In both Spain and Italy the Carthusian monasteries are in a class apart, and here, in this picturesque and weedgrown ruin, any traveller who, like myself, has loved the whiteclad monks of St. Bruno in so many more monasteries for their aristocratic seclusion, so unlike the dormitory life of the Cluniacs and Cistercians, will anticipate, or view in retrospect, Portacœli, on the coast below Valencia, with its cloisters, its precious marbles and paintings of the local school, overtaken by the fate of Poblet and of Santas Creus, but once the place in which to taste the gaiety and exuberance of the Levante; or Aula Dei, with its early frescoes by Goya, on a red ground, in the dust and glare of Zaragoza.

It was tempting to be told of Fuentebravía, on the coast,

where you could dine in the spring evening under a roof of boughs on prawns and lobsters freshly taken out of the darkening ocean, and to look from under the cedar tree where we were sitting, after luncheon with one of the *bodega* owners, at the white arum lilies growing in the resined shade. But the whole of this part of the coast, down to where I have walked on the sandy beach, strewn with shells, towards Tarifa, and seen a white town apparently round a headland just in front, and not known it was in Africa, across the Straits – this stretch of coast, in both directions, is beautiful in the extreme and fraught with history. There is Medina Sidonia inland, and with a name that, to an Englishman, must spell "Armada". Not far from there was the Phoenician Melkarth, sacked by Scipio Africanus, and Ford tells us – Livy is his authority – given by Scipio to the illegitimate children of Roman soldiers by Spanish mothers. Chiclana de la Frontera is a town of one-storeyed whitewashed houses with birdcage jalousies and a Gypsy suburb. Less than an hour further to the south by road, with the white towns of Africa coming ever nearer and nearer, lies Cape Trafalgar, and a little distance inland from that the veiled women of Vejer. These women are famous in Spain for the manner in which they are veiled, like nuns, from head to foot, the more impressively for the whitewashed courts they inhabit. They shroud their heads and faces, leaving but an eye visible, and perhaps a hand.[1] There can be no doubt that this is a living relic of Moorish rule. In the old pirate town of Sallee, across the estuary from Rabat, whence the Barbary corsairs sailed to the Bristol Channel, seized and held Lundy Island for some weeks, sacked Baltimore in Co. Cork, and on occasion raided as far north as Iceland, the women are veiled in just this manner, exceptionally even for Morocco. There is no difference but that at Sallee they are clothed in white from head to foot, like Carthusian or Cistercian nuns. When I wrote,

[1] Compare, also, the *tapadas*, veiled Spanish ladies of Lima, in Peru, promenading along the balconied streets in bright coloured cloaks or mantles, their heads shrouded, with but one eye showing. The *tapadas* are to be admired in old drawings of Lima, but are now no more. The "shocking-pink" of Schiaparelli is Peruvian in origin.

in a book on Morocco, that Sallee may be nearly the only town where such things are to be found close or contiguous to the ocean, for in the decline of Moslem power their centres of life and habit had retreated inland into the mountains or across the deserts, and that it is only at Sallee that they still rest upon the sea, I little knew that another band or sisterhood of Cyclop women was to be discovered in Spain, but in sight of Africa.

In the other direction, going north and passing Puerto de Santa María, where, in Ford's day, "the bull fights were perhaps the best in Spain", we would come to a humble fishing village with a famous name, Trocadero,[1] the syllables of which seem to spell of themselves a restaurant or night club and the clattering of plates and dishes somewhere not far from Piccadilly Circus. But a few miles further and we would come to Sanlúcar de Barrameda, at the mouth of the Guadalquivir, a little watering place to which Goya resorted in the summer of 1798, at a time when the Duchess of Alba was staying here. Two of his sketchbooks in the Prado, containing some of the most beautiful of his drawings of Andalucian *majos* and *majas*, and only lately published in their entirety, were the fruits of these journeys. Beyond lie the marshy plains of the Marismas, where only the seafowl and the cattle multiply; until, after fifty miles of the salt wilderness and within sight of Huelva, we would come to La Rábida, the Franciscan convent which not only gave refuge to Columbus, who sailed for the New World from the port of Palos nearby, but also sheltered Cortés on his return from Mexico.

A pair of the most fanciful and delightful of Andalucian towns are Carmona and Écija. Carmona, because of its whitewashed cleanliness and red brick houses has a curious Dutch quality, contradicted by its acacias and orange trees. It has wide streets, Moorish doorways, and a Roman landscape view over the Andalucian plain. Écija was a "discovery" made

---

[1] Trocadero was an outlying fort of Cádiz captured by the French army which traversed Spain in 1823, coming to the rescue of Ferdinand VII. Its commander was his cousin many times over, the Duc d'Angoulême. "Absolutism" was restored as a result of this curious campaign, coming so soon after Napoleon's wars in Spain.

by Théophile Gautier a hundred years ago, who wrote that he had arrived in a new country of pagodas and Hindu temples, with strange porcelain monuments and statues. The poet of *Mdlle de Maupin* is not exaggerating. There are other places besides Écija where there is something Hindu or East-Indian in the exuberant and prolix ornament of the southern architecture: in the great towers of El Obradoiro at Compostela, a façade and stairway that are nearly Cambodian; in the tiled domes of Murcia, Lorca, Orihuela, and other towns of the Levante; as in the golden façades of Lecce in southern Italy or the golden balconies of Noto in Sicily. Écija has three church towers faced with *azulejos* and several china monuments and fountains. It has the hottest climate of any town in Europe. Its country palaces are charming, particularly that of the Marqués de Peñaflor, with curving façade and windowboxes in full flower, doorway with Salomonic pillars, and Salomonic stairway. At Écija, Ford tells us, "some of the best bull fights in Spain take place", and we could wish to have been there a hundred years ago with him, in the dogdays of August, in the shadow of the china towers among the *sombreros* and *mantillas*. Écija, in fact, suggests Macao in China more than India, Macao when it was the home of the painter Chinnery; and remembering Écija we would like to accompany Ford or Gautier, or both, to other Andalucian towns, to Utrera or Osuna, where, in the words of the former, "the balconies of the houses are ornamented with superb carnation-pinks".

Another pair of towns which I would like to visit are Baeza and Úbeda. They are but five miles apart, up in the hills among the olive groves, near the mining town of Linares. The two towns are full of buildings of the early Renaissance, and in an old palace at Úbeda there has been installed the Parador Nacional del Condestable Dávalos, upon the same lines as the other Paradores that we have described in these pages. Baeza, from photographs, must have Plateresque and Renaissance façades in plenty; while Úbeda has Renaissance fountains, old churches, and Baeza, an old palace (of the Condes de Benavente) in what we would call the "tournament" style of Guadalajara, huge pilasters at either end with palm-like capitals that become balconies or *miradores*, a front with stones cut into facets, Gothic windows, and a long loggia or *mirador* of open arches, a palace worthy of Juan Güas and built, as surely, under his influence.

And now we are in the neighbourhood of one of the most spectacular of the Romerías. At the end of April and the beginning of September there is a Romería at the shrine of the Virgen de la Cabeza, in the Sierra Morena, but a few miles from Úbeda. A great many towns and villages make preparations for the pilgrimage and whole families and groups of friends take part. They set forth on horseback and in every sort of vehicle from as far as a hundred miles away towards the steep ascent of the Santuario, and encamp, the night before, on the hillside, beneath its walls. The Andalucian *majo* and *maja*, southern equivalents of the *charros* and *charras* of León and Old Castile, are to be seen in all their glory: spotted crinolines of Gypsy fashion for the women, Córdoban hats, short jackets, and tight trousers for the cavaliers, and there are dancing and music, all night, till dawn. Next morning, there is the procession of the crowned and jewelled image, the "Morenita", in midst of the beating of drums, the waving banners of the *cofradías* and the singing of *coplas*. The sanctuary of the Virgen de la Cabeza was almost completely destroyed during the Civil War, but has been rebuilt with a Parador attached to it, and the chief attraction of the Romería is the incomparable beauty of the landscape in which it takes place. It is one of the wildest regions of the Sierra Morena. Stags, wolves, wild boars, and lynxes roam the forests and the rocky crags and there are reports of *Capra hispanica*, the rarest game of all.

The Romería del Rocío is even more elaborate as a festival and like the Feria is one of the most beautiful survivals into this "utility", "dehydrated" age. It sets forth from Seville at Whitsun, and is to be seen making its way through the Gypsy suburb of Triana. The procession consists of a number of high, two-wheeled waggons drawn by pairs of oxen. First, a waggon which is a moving or nomad shrine, with a canopy of open pillars and many tiers of flowers and candles. Then, waggon after waggon with sides and roof of canvas, so that they are like tents on wheels, but this does not describe their shape, which is that of two-wheeled Gypsy caravans, "expressed", as dressmakers would say, not in wood but canvas. These waggon-tents are decorated and festooned, so that they resemble bowers, and the *majas* sit inside them with their shawls or spotted crinolines showing. Going at a slow pace through the Triana, among the excited population, there may be as many as forty or fifty of the waggons lumbering one after another, and the spectacle of so many tall, white, trembling tents or caravans approaching is one that has curious analogies, for it suggests, momentarily, the camel litters of the Holy Carpet setting off from Cairo through the desert on their way to Mecca. But these are pastoral ox waggons, and lovers of the past may recall engravings in old books on Constantinople and the Bosphorus of the *arrhubas* returning with the Sultan's women from picnics at the Sweet Waters of Asia. As it proceeds deeper into the country the Romería del Rocío is joined by other waggons, by the swift *charabán*, slow *carromato*, and roomy *tartana*, and by cavaliers in Andalucian costume who ride beside the wheels. There are, also, numbers of pilgrims on foot, carrying banners. The Romería lasts for three days, and they encamp beside their waggons. Perhaps it is never so beautiful as when passing under the grey shadow of the olive trees, tent after tent, with its occupants in their Gypsy dresses, and a horseman or two at the back, in stiff grey Córdoban hat and short white jacket, a young girl in a spotted crinoline riding pillion behind him. But it must be wonderful, too, at the evening encampments, when they sing and dance far into the night. And, indeed, song and dance, blazing days, and starlit nights are the attractions of the Romería.

2

Castile and Aragon

1. GOTHIC SPAIN

Toledo Cathedral – Salamanca – Valladolid – Guadalajara –
Zamora – León – Santiago de Compostela

THERE is the clanking of heavy keys. Various *canónigos,*
roused from their midday siesta or from talking where they
foregather at the *farmacia*, take a last pinch of snuff and gather
at the appointed hour from different quarters of the immense
church. Is is the hour when the treasury of Toledo cathedral
is opened to the public.

Always, and on every occasion, it is too early or too late,
for there is so much to see that one is tired long before it is
time for the treasury to open. There are the *Coro*, the *Capilla
Mayor*, the *Trasparente;* there are the *Salas Capitulares*, the
summer and winter chapter houses, the *Sacristía,* the *Vestuario*, the *Ropería*, and the *Ochavo*. There are the *Capilla Mozárabe*, the *Capilla de Santiago*, and those of the *Reyes Nuevos* and of *San Ildefonso*, not to mention other objects beyond
number, including the stained glass windows, which used to be
magnificent but were much damaged in the Civil War, when
the cathedral and the greater part of its contents escaped by
a miracle; but the Reds murdered some eighty of the wretched
priests and canons.

Toledo cathedral, like Seville, León, Burgos, is a thirteenth
century French building. In plan it even bears a close resemblance to Notre Dame de Paris. But we are standing in front
of the Capilla Mayor admiring the grille, or *reja*, of gilt metal,
which is beyond words magnificent, the work of Francesco
de Villalpando and one of the most notable triumphs of the
Spanish ironsmiths. The Capilla Mayor was built by Cardinal
Ximenes, in the cold words of the guide book, "without

73

disturbing the coffins of the kings and archbishops buried below", and the gilt *retablo* by Enrique de Egas is only inferior to that of Seville. The Coro is not less splendid than the Capilla Mayor and has an astonishing display of woodcarving in its eighty choir stalls, of which number fifty seats and five flights of steps of walnut wood with contemporary reliefs of the conquest of Granada are by Rodrigo Alemán, most interesting for their Moorish costumes; but that German sculptor has not here given free rein to his medieval imagination, as in the wild and licentious woodcarvings of the stalls of Plasencia; while the rest of the Toledo choir stalls are the work of the Burgundian Felipe Vigarni and of Alonso Berruguete.

Three chapels in splendid late flamboyant Gothic recall the Capilla del Condestable at Burgos, and bring us back again to that strange world of satyrs or "wild men" and of heralds in embroidered tabards like the knaves from packs of playing cards. The first, immediately behind the high altar, is the Capilla de San Ildefonso, full of tombs; next to it is the Capilla de Santiago, built in the form of a hexagon by the Condestable Don Álvaro de Luna. This knight, who was beheaded by his king, lies, in marble, in full armour with his wife by his side and his sword between his legs, with four knights of Santiago in hauberk mail kneeling at the corners. Ford tells us in his Handbook that "under these tombs there exists a vault, which had to be repaired at the beginning of (last) century. The workmen who entered it said that the skeletons of Don Álvaro and his wife were seated at a table, the head of Don Álvaro being placed before him." The third chapel is that of the Reyes Nuevos, more Plateresque than Gothic, with a pair of armed heralds at the entrance, and many tombs of kings and queens, including that the Plantagenet Catalina Alencastre,[1] daughter of John of Gaunt.

Now comes the great Salón de la Sacristía containing the *Expolio*, by El Greco, paintings by Goya and other masters, and a painted ceiling by Luca Giordano. This is a trick work by that facile painter. In the morning a beam of sunlight

[1] We write the name thus, in medieval form, because it is a reminder of the still flourishing Portuguese families of this descent.

shines across the ceiling from the figure of the Almighty. Nevertheless it is one of the best works of "fa Presto", not forgetting his ceiling painting at the Palazzo Riccardi at Florence of the Medici as gods of light among the deities of Olympus, or his "non-stop" frescoes, completed in forty-eight hours on his return from Spain, while the Sacrament was kept exposed, on the dome of the treasury at the Certosa di San Martino, above Naples. Indeed, as a painted interior of the late seventeenth century it compares favourably with the white horses of Solimena at the two ends of the sacristy of San Paolo Maggiore, the church which still has the classical portico of a temple of Castor and Pollux as its entrance, also in Naples.

Out of this Salón de la Sacristía lead the Ochavo (Octagon), built by the son of El Greco, an undistinguished architect, containing many treasures, and the Vestuario and the Ropería, with their embroidered vestments, probably the greatest collection of such textiles in the Occidental world, if we except the Old Ecclesiastical Treasury in the Kremlin. There are complete sets in crimson or green velvet of the sixteenth century; vestments made from the robes of earlier kings which are like the figures from playing cards in terms of heraldry; sundry Portuguese and other banners, including that hung from the galley of Don Juan of Austria at the battle of Lepanto (and which is still hung from the transept of the cathedral on the first Sunday in October, the anniversary of that battle); and tent hangings of gold twine worked with the arms and motto of los Reyes Católicos, Ferdinand and Isabella. The Tesoro Mayor at the far end of the cathedral, to which we may imagine that the canons are now making their way, glitters and coruscates with gold and silver, and by dint of long explanation is not a little tiring. Few persons will have energy still to admire the immense silver *custodia* of Enrique de Arfe or to delay more than reflectively at the Capilla Mozárabe, wherein the Visigothic ritual is still celebrated daily.[1]

But we will end our tour of Toledo cathedral on a less solemn and more frivolous note, for which our thanks are due to the much derided and abused Narciso Tomé, sculptor or

[1] As in six of the parish churches of Toledo until 1851.

architect (or he could as well be called author or choreograph) of the celebrated Trasparente. This theatrical *trompe l'oeil* made permanent is staged immediately behind the high altar. Its subject – and this can be said, too, in terms of the theatre or the ballet – is the gift of the Holy Communion to mankind, a belated but none the less effective protest against Jansen and the Northern heretics. Narciso Tomé, with a deft hand and greatly daring, has broken through the stone vaulting of the roof and let in a golden light. This opening, which he has contrived into a cupola, and the stucco masking of a pair of the original Gothic piers, has given him sufficient space to create this extraordinary illusion, in which we see, in marble and in stucco, the angels and seraphim, a seated figure of Christ in glory, the Virgin ascending to heaven, the Last Supper, and among the subsidiary host San Rafael who so offended Richard Ford, in his own words, "head downwards, with his legs kicking out above him in the air, and holding in his right hand a huge *gilt* fish". Ford continues, justly, that the Trasparente "in spite of its absurdities, evinces much invention, and great workmanship and mastery over material". It is, in fact, an extreme instance of the Baroque *pièce montée* in the tradition descending from Bernini's Ecstasy of St. Teresa, in Rome,[1] and of which the works of the brothers Asam in Bavaria are examples, and with *El Obradoiro* (the western façade of the cathedral of Santiago de Compostela) and with the façade of the cathedral at Murcia it is one of the outstanding achievements of Baroque art in Spain. The Trasparente was dedicated in 1732, with great rejoicings and a bull fight, and Fray Francisco Rodríguez Galán thought fit to celebrate the occasion with a poem, *Octava maravilla cantada en octavas rimas*.

If there be no cathedral in Spain that is so full of treasures as Toledo, there are others that are little less extraordinary in their accumulation of works of art and that may be more interesting architecturally. The Spanish cathedrals are, indeed, something apart in the history of the arts of Europe, and in their rôle of storehouses, or sacred repositories we learn to

[1] Santa Maria della Vittoria.

expect of them certain qualities which are absent, or were never present, in the restored and ravaged cathedrals of France and England, or in the Italian *duomo*. How often, in memory, have we not found ourselves in front of some gilt *retablo*, remembered some golden organ case towering half-way to the height of the nave, levelling at us, but far over our heads, its broadsides and batteries of gilded pipes, or recalled the tomb of some forgotten lady or young knight; have had the sudden or instantaneous image of all or any of these and not, for the moment, been able to remember who or what they were ! Are these the carved and gilded compartments of Toledo or Seville, with figures crowding in upon one another and reaching to the vaulting? Is this the *retablo* of San Nicolás at Burgos, by Francisco de Colonia, or do we recognize the figures of Don Juan II and Queen Isabella kneeling in the corners and, looking up to the carved pelican feeding its young, know that it is the *retablo* of the Cartuja de Miraﬂores, by Gil de Silóee? Are those the double organ cases, one each side of the *coro,* of Granada cathedral; the Moor's head with beard of real hair and painted cheeks hanging under the organ of Barcelona, and facing towards the cloister of the sacred geese; or the musical artillery, the salvos and broadsides, of Córdoba, where the organ cases tower like twin temples by the Bibienas among the double horseshoe arches of the Moorish mosque? Here, at least, is the tomb of the *Doncel,* a king's page or young knight, Don Martín Vázquez de Arce, killed before Granada. His tomb is in the family chapel at Sigüenza and it is impossible to mistake him, for he leans on an elbow, reading or reciting poetry to himself, as he has done since 1486. His effigy by an unknown sculptor has the cap and short cloak and long hose of a youth of the end of the fifteenth century, when a new and Italian poetry was in the air, and seeing the repose of this young knight and agreeing that his is one of the most beautiful sculptures in Spain, in that beautifully far, remote cathedral away in the endless, interminable red plains, thinking of that dawning poetry to which he was born and died and of that new world of fact and of the imagination, contrasting the European Renaissance with our own fallen hopes and

77

anticipation of nothing but more, and still more ugliness up to the final and crepuscular explosion, we must envy the *Doncel* his long sleep and wish for him that, as in his effigy, he is not so much asleep as dreaming with the new poetry upon his lips.

The thought of that tomb, and of the young knight reclining upon it in sempiternal silence – never to be disturbed, we hope, till it is as old as the stone statues of the ancients, till maybe the arts have come down again upon the earth – is enough to start us journeying over the high plateau in search of some other of the cathedrals that are so typical of Spain. We are at a point, therefore, where the tawny domes and spires of Salamanca first make themselves visible out of the plain, and before long in full view of the great golden churches we are crossing the Roman bridge of many arches into the town.

In point of architecture Salamanca is one of the wonders of Europe. Nowhere else are there to be seen so many Gothic buildings of the richest period of Ferdinand and Isabella, a style "tainted", as some authorities would have it, by the Manoeline of nearby Portugal; but it is, in reality a Gothic with a peculiar Romanticism all its own. And there are, as well, the Oriental-looking "beehive" cupolas of the Old Cathedral and superb buildings of the later Renaissance, together with works by various of the Churriguera family that belie their name. Salamanca is, indeed, the town of the Churrigueras. Even so, the greater number of the churches and colleges of Salamanca were destroyed during the Napoleonic wars, or in the words of Wellington himself, "the French among other acts of violence have destroyed 13 out of 25 convents, and 20 out of 25 colleges which existed in this celebrated seat of learning". The western half of the town thus perished. The New Cathedral, which adjoins the Old, is the late Gothic work of Juan Gil de Hontañón, and it has portals or, rather, flat, ornamented entrances of utmost magnificence carved with statues, busts, medallions, and coats-of-arms in the creamy golden stone of Salamanca, which takes ornament, and hardens, like the stone of the Baroque towns of Lecce and of Noto in the Two Sicilies. Such carvings, which are as rich as tapestries or needlework, are a feature of Salamanca. The interior of the New Cathedral and its sacristy, with "lustres de Venise" and mirrors, and its "aspect d'une salle de bal", owes much of its coloured decoration to Joaquín and Alberto Churriguera, two sprigs of the notorious family.

A few steps lead down into the Old Cathedral, where the air is solemn and more beautiful. There is, in particular, the chapel of the Anaya family, leading out of the cloisters, with the tomb of an archbishop of Seville in the centre, enclosed in a splendid railing. Ladies and knights of the Anaya family lie all round the walls; among others, an armed knight and his lady dressed like a nun, the costume which she wore while her husband was at the wars, and it is impossible not to be moved by the memory of these gentlemen and these ladies and not to wonder whether the blood of the Anayas still flows in any Spanish family, or whether this chapel and the dead quiet is all that is left to them. In a corner of the chapel is an organ of the early sixteenth century. There can be nothing like this. It is purely medieval, with Mudéjar ornament, one of the most romantic, poetical objects imaginable. It is possible to climb a few rungs up the ladder, to nearly above the Mudéjar gallery. What music was played upon it? More still, with what music were its player and his audience familiar, as dead now as the Anaya family lying in their stone coffins all around?

But it is the roofs and cupolas of the Old Cathedral that are its interest architecturally, for they are in a manner of Oriental-Romanesque that some authorities would call Périgourdin, and trace to Périgueux; while others would connect it, by reason of Jerónimo of Périgueux, almoner of the Cid, who became bishop of Salamanca and Zamora, with some French architect who had seen the Norman domes of Amalfi and the church of La Martorana at Palermo, or with the lantern of the church of the Holy Sepulchre at Jerusalem, the work of Frenchmen. The "fish scale" stone tiles of Salamanca are typical of the Romanesque school of Poitiers. As an architectural feature the lantern of the Old Cathedral of Salamanca can be allowed many origins. The interior of the lantern, with its double row of columns and round arches and its melon ribs, is as Oriental as its exterior spire, with the "fish scale" tiles that suggest, also, the Tartar armour of sliced horses' hooves. Dates, however, make it extremely unlikely that there was any influence from the church of St. Front at Périqueux, while close personal acquaintance with Palermo, and with Amalfi and Ravello, fails to detect any similarity to the domes of Salamanca. It can, therefore, have been but a contemporary Oriental influence in the air, connected probably with tales of the Holy Sepulchre at Jerusalem and with an admiration for the buildings of the Saracens. The church at Toro, forty miles from Salamanca, has another of the Romanesque lanterns, with beautiful window openings and little round turrets at the corners, while perhaps the most wonderful instance of all is at Zamora.

One of the richest specimens of the Isabelline or Plateresque in Spain is the façade of the University at Salamanca. This, again, is a flat screen suggesting a tapestry or needlework or even a stupendously elaborate stamped bookbinding. The medallions, coats-of-arms, and grotesques are magnificent in execution, and in a style related to the "Hospital façades" of Santa Cruz at Toledo and of the Royal Hospital at Santiago de Compostela, and to the tremendous stamped and incised "fronts" of San Pablo and San Gregorio at Valladolid, except that the two latter are late Gothic, entirely, in inspiration and owe nothing to the Renaissance. But they are identical in purpose or, rather, in lack of that, for the interiors are mere decoration. There are, in fact, two sorts of Plateresque, Gothic and Renaissance. The Gothic Plateresque, as Mr. Bernard Bevan remarks, "seems to have originated in the exuberant taste of the Flemings, Germans, and Burgundians working in Burgos and in Toledo". In the next generation Plateresque was the work not of foreigners but of Spaniards, and it becomes Italian or Renaissance in feeling. At Valladolid – for this is our opportunity to delay there – the two "fronts" of San Gregorio and of San Pablo, considered together, take on a new pretence or influence, for they are pretending to be not architectural frontispieces but carved *retablos*. The units or "limbs" of the "front" of San Pablo are those, exactly, of

9   Toledo cathedral: El Trasparente, by Narciso Tomé, 1732

11   Ronda: the gorge and Roman bridge

10   Segovia: the fifteenth-century castle of Coca

12 Zamora: the dome of the cathedral (late twelfth century)

13 Toledo cathedral: the west front (1418-44)

14 Seville: procession of hooded penitents during Holy Week

15 History of Tarquin: "Black" Tapestry of Zamora
(fifteenth century, woven at Arras)

16 Salamanca: Charra costumes

the wooden compartments of a *retablo*; but San Gregorio – attributed to Juan Güas, who came from Lyons[1] – is more fantastic still, while its *patio* is pure fantasy. It is the "Espagnolade" of a foreigner, as much so as the drawings of Gustave Doré or the music of Carmen.

The central panel of the *retablo* front of San Gregorio, over the archway, consists of a huge shield with the royal arms upheld by supporters standing in the branches of a tree, which, in its turn, shoots up from out a fountain. They are "wild men" or satyrs, and the cresting or battlementing is of broken twigs. But the *patio* is a still more extraordinary affair, verging on the Manoeline of Portugal. It is Moorish or "Indian" in influence, widely interpreted, for this is not the current Mudéjar of the day. Mr. Bernard Bevan writes of its architect, Juan Güas, that "like the sculptor Juni (Jean) de Joigny" (d. 1586, whose "mannerist" works, much influenced by Michael Angelo, are to be seen in the museum of sculpture in the Colegio de San Gregorio in this very city of Valladolid), "and like the painter El Greco, he is an example of the extent to which the Spanish temperament, outlook, and taste captivated foreign artists". Juan Güas was architect, also, of San Juan de los Reyes in Toledo, the church which Ferdinand and Isabella had intended for their burial place until the conquest of Granada. This is the *nec plus ultra* of late Gothic, with huge shields of heraldry and decorated Gothic lettering in the frieze recalling the Moorish inscriptions in the Alhambra, but nothing else "Indian" or Manoeline in its fantasy, a vein which Juan Güas reserved for the interior *patio* of San Gregorio.

Returning to Salamanca after an obligatory glance at the fantastic buildings of Valladolid, in all other respects an unattractive city, we find ourselves standing in the Plaza Mayor, looking round at its arcades and balconies, and the Ayuntamiento, the work of two of the Churrigueras and of another

[1] Other authorities have it that Juan Güas was Jan Was, a Dutchman or a Fleming, though Mr Bernard Bevan points out that Guasch is still quite a common Catalan name to be found in the telephone books of Barcelona. Perhaps, then, the name is Catalan in origin and Guas but another Catalan "original", like Gaudí and Salvador Dalí!

architect, Quiñones, probably the most beautiful example of a public square in Spain. Bull fights were held here within the last hundred years. And continuing past the enormous and theatrical Seminario Conciliar, with its splendid interior courts or cloisters, we come to the Casa de las Conchas, of pure fantasy yet one of the most "Spanish" things in Spain. Its exterior, as the name portends, is studded with carved scallop shells, a form of decoration that is, after all, no more unreasonable than the rustication of the Palazzo Strozzi in Florence, one of the admitted masterworks of the Italian Renaissance. If the Casa de las Conchas was really completed in 1483 and not, as some authorities would have it, in 1514, it antedated its Florentine equivalent. Moreover, its wrought iron lanterns and lovely triple window grille might be held to surpass in beauty the more famous *fanali* or corner lanterns of the Palazzo Strozzi, which are among the most celebrated instances of Italian ironwork of the time. The window grilles have been conceived especially for the shadows that they throw, which are like so many intricate cages hanging on the golden stone. Within there is a beautiful *patio*, less extreme than, though akin to, that of San Gregorio at Valladolid.

If we would pursue this same vein of Spanish fantasy into its ultimate expression we have to recreate for ourselves the much damaged palace of the Dukes of Infantado at Guadalajara, on the other side of Madrid, upon the line to Aragon. When I saw this, some fifteen years ago, I thought it the strangest and most poetic building I had ever seen: poetical in the direct sense, as though a poet had designed it. But it is, in fact, by Juan Güas (and his brother), architect of San Gregorio at Valladolid, with its *retablo* façade and curious *patio*, and of San Juan de las Reyes at Toledo. The façade of golden stone is studded with carved knobs or facets and over the door there hangs an immense shield-of-arms with satyr supporters. Like the Casa de las Conchas, the Infantado palace is not large compared with palaces in Italy. The cornice of this strange building is formed of a double row of stalactites, and it is at this stage that we may believe the theory that a Moor called Egüaomit was also employed upon it, for above that there is an open gallery of Moorish looking windows with balconies or semicircular *miradores* at intervals. It was from these *miradores* that François I, held prisoner after the battle of Pavia, looked down upon the tournaments held in his honour by the Duque del Infantado. François I looked down, and knowing his proclivities we may feel certain there were handsome ladies in his company. But it is when François I, in his plumed cap, his jewels and slashed sleeves, withdraws from those masthead galleries into the palace of the Mendozas that we would follow him. It is two-storeyed, with lions "that have heads like hedgehogs" over the arches, scrolls, and mottoes of its *patio*, and a rich balcony. Certain of the rooms – for we must revert alas! to the past tense – had chimneypieces and ceilings of indescribable magnificence, surely the finest and most romantic things of their kind in Europe. The most beautiful of the rooms were below the balconies, upon the upper floor; the Salón de Cazadores (hunters) with a gilded ceiling unsurpassed for beauty, and the Salón de Linajes (genealogies) with stalactite frieze, carved figures of satyrs, and an *artesonado* ceiling of the type that is inlaid with *lacería*, or flat patterns. According to tradition this had been François I's bedroom, and it was hung with a hundred coats-of-arms of the hundred best pedigrees in Spain. All these ceilings must have been the work of Mudéjar carpenters, who were the most consummate of craftsmen in this respect. The ceilings of this Renaissance, this Manoeline, this Moorish palace, where a King of France was prisoner and where Philip II was married to Isabelle of Valois, are not less beautiful in execution than the exquisite wooden and gilt stalactite or honeycomb vaulting and *media naranja* dome to the porch of the mosque of Bou Medine, outside Tlemcen, in Algeria, which is the best work of the Moors in North Africa, not exceeded in fanciful delicacy and precision by any works of the Mughals in India, or of Persian craftsmen in Meshed or Isfahan. Unfortunately, the Infantado palace, which had become an orphanage and was run by nuns, was fearfully injured in a street battle in 1936. This was the most dreadful artistic casualty of the Spanish Civil War, a loss which is irreparable and complete.

We come back, once more, to Salamanca, architecturally the most interesting and beautiful of Spanish cities – with finer buildings than Toledo or Seville, but without the situation of one or the associations and gaiety of the other – in order to stress its extraordinary continuity down the ages and its wealth of buildings; although, as we have seen, half of the town perished in the Napoleonic wars. Activity has returned to it. It is now a busy, cheerful place. Twenty years ago it was different, and I shall never forget the pitying face of the French sleeping car attendant, a Parisian, when the night express from Lisbon halted at Salamanca at one o'clock in the morning and he handed me my luggage, and told me I should soon be wishing I had continued on my journey. In addition to its buildings of the Isabelline period there are the works of the Churrigueras to be separated and disentangled, a task which has never yet been done: José Churriguera himself, his brothers, and three children. And opposite the church of San Esteban, built for Dominican monks in High Renaissance, there is perhaps the most tempting mystery left in Spain, the convent of Las Dueñas (Dominicas de Santa María), in strictest *clausura*, of which not even photographs are available, but known to contain Mudéjar *patios* and ceilings, and works of art which may excel those kept in perpetual *clausura* in Tordesillas and Astudillo.

We now leave Salamanca, going northwards over the endless plains into the old Kingdom of León. And we stay for the night at the Albergue de la Bañeza, exactly half-way on the high road from Madrid to La Coruña, one of the new road-houses, built and owned by the Dirección General del Turismo, the emergence of which hostelries in their improbable setting is excuse enough for a description. For some time before reaching it, late on a spring evening, the ancient town of Benavente had appeared and disappeared like a mirage in and behind the salt lagoons. Then came low hills, not higher than mounds, with row after row of little conical chimneys projecting from their summits. And in a few moments we were passing whole villages of wine cellars with stout wooden doors down little tunnels dug into the hillside. In the golden light they looked like Indian *pueblos* in New Mexico. The kilometre posts along the road got nearer and nearer to the 300 mark (the exact distance of the Albergue from Madrid and 305 kilometres to La Coruña) and just beyond the village of La Bañeza, not more than a hundred yards from the given location, a low, whitewashed building came into sight. All the Albergues are built to the same pattern so that the Albergue de la Bañeza may be taken as typical of all the others. Their purpose is to provide shelter and accommodation, where none is to be had, at strategic points along the highroads, at halfway from Madrid to the coast, as here, or where there is some particular attraction in the way of antiquities or scenery. They contain a small sitting-room, a dining-room of semicircular form where excellent food is served at all hours of the day and deep into the Spanish night; while upstairs there are usually eight bedrooms, four double and four single, with wire netting over the windows, and bathrooms. Behind the Albergue there are a garage and petrol pump, and in front a terrace and a kitchen garden. This modest accommodation is kept scrupulously clean; and with previous memories of nights spent in provincial towns in Spain, it was a sensation bordering on the incredible to dine in this bright and modern setting, take down an old landscape annual on Andalucía or an early Victorian book on the *fiestas* of Seville from the little library, and then go to bed and lie awake for a time listening to the nightingales. The mere sensation of being out of the town and in the country is a blessing in itself. But, as well, there is the certainty of a clean bedroom and a comfortable bed.

My one thought while falling asleep was to continue to the Albergue de Puebla de Sanabria, in a still more remote place only some fifteen miles from the frontier of Portugal, a village which may be looked for in vain in any modern guide book, but Ford speaks of it as lying "a two-days' journey over the mountains in a fine wild country, covered with aromatic underwood". He tells of its "magnificent views of the Vierzo and Asturian chain, extending from the Galician mountains to the Picos de Europa", and of its fishing grounds, among the best in all Spain, including the famous lake of San Martín de Castañeda, "a crystal loch like the filled crater of a volcano, about 4 miles round, and of unknown depth . . . hemmed in by the spurs of the slaty and often snowclad hills. The trout are noble in size, inexhaustible in number, and when in season pink as chars." He tells of "the monasteries and trout streams of Vierzo", of "old abbeys and sheikh-shepherds who fed their flocks upon the thyme-clad hills", for this fertile and beautiful valley, shut out, as it were, from the world, and little known even in our own day in spite of its old Mozarabic churches, was once a second Thebaid and rivalled the holiest districts of Palestine in the number of its hermits, "whom God alone, who can count the stars of heaven, could enumerate". Of a village upon the way Ford remarks: "Here girls await the diligence with tumblers of delicious new milk and glasses of water", and with him for guide we approach the chief town of the Vierzo, "placed as in a funnel of mountains with cottages, convents, vines, balconies, and painterlike bridges hanging over the trout streams". It is but twenty miles from Puebla de Sanabria over the mountains to Bragança, the cradle of the family of that name, through country which must be some of the wildest in all Europe, and trackless even now; and taking up another book, the French *Guide Bleu* to Portugal, for a last moment before turning out the light, we read of Mudéjar ceilings and stalactite friezes, of a race of forgotten crypto-Jews who were only discovered after the first war, and of the Serra do Montezinho where flocks numbering more than a million are pastured during the summer, and there are stags and wild boars in the pine forest. The Sierra de la Culebra, nearer still, has its particular patois (*mirandês*), and among the peculiar customs of the inhabitants are funeral feasts and "le rapt de mariées". They wear hoods (*capuchones*) and cloaks made of strips of different coloured bunting, and perform the *dança dos paulitos,* and have a famous breed of cattle, and . . . and . . .

Not too early next morning – for in Spain it is never necessary to start the day at sunrise and you soon learn to make a practice of arriving in the middle of the night – we were on the road to Zamora. This is a town I have wished to visit all the knowledgeable years of my life because of the tapestries belonging to the cathedral, and in the achievement it is not a disappointment. The old town, much modernized and with good shops, stands on the Duero, which, later, becomes the Douro and forms the frontier with Portugal for some sixty miles before turning to flow down through the vines of Trás-os-Montes. Could we continue further we would see the port wine brought down to the river in ox carts by peasant women in round tambour hats and the *capa de honras*, a cloak or mantle of parti-coloured cloth worn with a great hood, and the golden jewellery of Gondomar, and being loaded on board the *rabelos*, wine boats with square lateen sails and gigantic rudders worked by a helmsman standing on a high platform at the back, and so float down slowly to Oporto. Perhaps Zamora is so typical of Spain that it must be near the end of all things Spanish, but certainly no towns are more Spanish, as we hope to show, than Mérida, Cáceres, Trujillo, Plasencia, that are along the frontier with Portugal. It is therefore the more mysterious that in Zamora the things that are unique are importations and not of the Spaniards at all.

The cathedral has a lantern dome in the manner of Salamanca, in strange and peculiar Oriental style, which yet cannot be called Byzantine, a melon dome, and four little turrets with pilasters and domes around it that are complete little Oriental creations of the shape, almost, of Saracenic helmets, the whole influenced, there can be small doubt, by the church of the Holy Sepulchre at Jerusalem. It is with a breath of Aleppo or Damascus that we go into the cathedral, but all memory of the interior is obliterated by the tapestries. They are displayed in some rooms upstairs in the cloister. This marvellous experience, that is comparable to a personal re-creation of the Middle Ages, begins upon the stone staircase, on one wall of which there hangs loosely an immense black tapestry of the History of Tarquin. The use of black is as strong in it, and as all-pervading, as the rose-coloured ground in the Cluny tapestries of the Lady and the Unicorn, and it should be given the name of the Black Tapestry of Zamora.

The first details we see, coming up the staircase, are a pair of black rat-tail shoes; and then a black-clad archer standing immediately before us, the size of life, with thin legs and figure, drawing his bow obliquely out of the tapestry; and the white neck of a horse with braided mane and bridle, and an entire battle in progress. Then, at the other corner, the tapestry being divided into three subjects or compartments, we see a lady on a white horse riding forward, a few feet away from us, in a flowering meadow by the walls and turrets of a Gothic town. She rides in a concourse of horsemen, with mounted pages or esquires, another young lady on horseback, and a page on foot who holds a banner. It is Tanaquilda, the wife of Tarquin; her husband appears in the middle foreground, in armour, with the eagle of legend hovering above his head. And now we see more and more horsemen coming out of the folds of the tapestry, one of them wearing a long cloak and riding a charger which has curvetted round and turned its hindquarters to us; it is a long black cloak trimmed with gold, the horses' hooves are treading the spring flowers, and now we see a page on foot with long fair hair holding the bridle for Tanaquilda, her two dogs with shaggy coats; and in the centre the crowning of Tarquin under a canopy, many nobles with black caps, black shoes, and long, thin black legs, and at his feet the masons, clod on shoulder, building the walls and aqueducts of Rome. This tapestry of the History of Tarquin is of the highest possible quality. It is equal to the most superb Gothic tapestries extant, probably from the looms of Tournai, and there is a clue to its origin when we know that black was the colour worn by the courtiers of the Dukes of Burgundy.

The tapestries of the Wars of Troy are in the rooms above. There are four panels at Zamora out of a set that consisted originally of eleven hangings. These are a little earlier than the History of Tarquin, of Tournai manufacture, too, but not quite so fine in execution. They are a little clumsy and confused in drawing, and in their predominance of red and gold one misses those tremendous blacks. They are, however, marvellous in detail, by accumulation of detail as we might call it. The tapestries do not run consecutively, being the second, fifth, seventh, and eleventh of the series. In the first we have the expedition of the Trojans to Greece and the Rape of Helen, and are haunted by memories of the great medieval ship in the middle with its mast and rigging rising to the height of the panel, and by the curious sailor crouched on board, bearded and in a peaked hood, casting off the rope which another sailor is untying, an inch or two away, on shore. The beauty of these incredible tapestries is enhanced by the long inscriptions in chivalric, rhyming French of the Middle Ages at the top of each panel.[1]

In the Tent of Achilles, the second tapestry, the background is a battle scene as crowded as the battle pictures of Uccello. The knights' lances and their shields and banners fill the background and form a veritable forest through which we can see the faces of the ladies looking down on the battle from the walls of Troy. It is the convention of the French carved ivories of the thirteenth century where the ladies are watching a tournament from the turrets of a castle. The tent is in the foreground. The white charger of Achilles stands at the tent door, a magnificent animal with white curving mane and long white tail held by a page who wears the most elegant of pointed shoes. Another white charger is behind him, close to a palisade of vines growing on a bare space of wall below a corbelled turret, while the tent itself is full of Greeks and Orientals, as the artist conceived of them, wearing the most richly embroidered brocades and velvets, every accoutrement and jewel rendered in detail, and bearing evidence in their beards and high, peaked fur caps, like those of Russian boyars, that the artist had in mind the costumes of Byzantine nobles. These Greek knights with their dark hair, their curving scimitars and jewelled robes, can only be intended for courtiers of the Palaeologi. In the other corner a knight on horseback, fully caparisoned, rides forth to battle, while above him in a castle room there is a group of exquisite young ladies in brocaded robes and fabulous headdresses.

The remaining pair of tapestries, the deaths of Troilus, Achilles, and Paris, are stupendous battle scenes containing

[1] And in "dog-Latin" at the bottom.

hundreds of jostling figures. The wooden horse, as richly caparisoned as any rajah's elephant, is ridden in through the shattered walls by a knight with strongly marked Oriental features and wearing an extravagantly high fur hat. There are ships curved like Venetian gondolas riding at anchor below the walls, and the ruins are in flower, for wherever you look there are wild flowers growing in the middle of the battle. The whole edge of this tapestry where the walls are breached is a high turret. A Greek knight rides through the breach, and his pages are treading with their pointed shoes a whole thicket of wild roses. Merely as a fabric these tapestries of the Wars of Troy are richer than the Persian "hunting" carpets. Alone, in themselves, they are worth the visit to Zamora, and it must sadden every lover of the arts to look for the last time at the Wars of Troy and then, with mind attuned to that crowded and tumultuous poetry, to those endless battles among the flowers, come down the stairway past the History of Tarquin, by the black bowman, by Queen Tanaquilda on her white horse, by the nobles and pages all in black, and so out into the modern world.

It is about seventy miles further on over the mountains to Astorga, once the capital city of the Maragatos, a people of uncertain origin, who live in thirty-six villages in the country round and still migrate to Madrid as muleteers and vendors of fish, but no longer wear their peculiar costume of long skirted coats and kneebreeches, and meet no more in the market-place of Astorga at Corpus Christi and at Ascension to perform their dance of *El Cañizo*. Astorga is a dreary town with a cathedral that has elaborate Gothic portals recalling Tudor Gothic, as is remarked by Mr. Bernard Bevan, with a façade by Gil de Hontañón, architect of the Catedral Nueva at Salamanca, and of the cathedral at Segovia, but if there is occasion to delay further in this little town it is only in order to wait for the hour to strike above the Rococo Ayuntamiento, for this is struck by two painted wooden figures of a Maragato and a Maragata. This used to give the signal for the dance to start, "beginning at two o'clock in the afternoon and ending at three exactly", to be broken off immediately if anyone not a Maragato tried to join,[1] and we can look up at the painted figures and see the only remaining traces of the Maragato costume, the baggy breeches of the man and the short skirt and slashed sleeves of the woman with her heavy jewellery hung with reliquaries that suggests the Berber origin of this curious people.

The last stretches of the plain between Astorga and León, and it is not long before the towers of the cathedral of León rise out of the poplars along the pale green valley. The cathedral is entirely French Gothic; it stands in an ugly square of modern buildings; the interior has been conscientiously cleared of all Renaissance or Baroque additions, and apart from the magnificent array of stained glass windows rivalling those of Bourges, León cathedral is a stranger among the splendours and wonders of old Spain. It may be the most perfect example of Gothic in the peninsula, but it could stand too easily in a French provincial town. It is, in contrast, like a breath of Spanish music to stand in front of the convent of San Marcos, a golden and magnificent example of the Spanish Plateresque, where pilgrims were sheltered on their way to and from Santiago de Compostela. It is now a barracks. The ancient and chivalric glory of León has ebbed and flowed away; nor do the stone coffins of eleven early kings, twelve queens, and twenty-one princes or grandees in San Isidoro bespeak the living past. Twenty miles from León is the tenth century Mozarabic church of San Miguel de Escalada, which I have not visited, but which is the most beautiful building of the early Gothic Kingdoms left in Spain, built by monks from Córdoba who arrived in León speaking Arabic, and betrayed their origin in the twelve arches of the portico and the palm frond capitals and horseshoe arches of the interior, a Christian church that has, therefore, much of the aspect of an early mosque in Kairouan and is not the less curious in the cold winds of León.

But León and Asturias are the regions of Spain that are

[1] When Mr. Royall Tyler was in Astorga, "the Maragatos were making a noise with their castanets that can be heard at the distant railway station." Cf. *Spain*, by Royall Tyler, 1909, p. 192. There are fourteen more regional costumes in León alone.

most rich in early buildings. Outside the coal and iron town of Oviedo, upon the green hillside and mercifully removed from its blackening embraces, are the two churches, hardly a hundred yards apart, of San Miguel de Lino and Santa María de Naranco. They were built in the ninth century by Ramiro I, King of the Asturias, contemporary, therefore, with our Saxon kings. San Miguel de Lino, which suggests a church in Armenia or Georgia, has carved panels in its doorway that are copied from Byzantine consular ivories, though post-dating those by three centuries. Santa María de Naranco is said by some authorities to have been built by Ramiro for his summer villa. It has beautiful open porticos at both ends, recalling the much later porches of the Pantanassa, at Mistra in the Peloponnese. The buttresses are other architectural features, and the building contains two churches, an upper and a lower, but compared with the Mozarabic San Miguel de Escalada this is entirely Christian. It is Eastern Christian, but has nothing of Córdoba or North Africa. In point of artistic value this small building, whether church or Villa, is to be preferred to the bare bones of León and is important evidence as to the aesthetic beauty of the early kingdoms. Whether it was his summer villa or not, it stood near to the baths and gardens of Ramiro, and it is in such a setting that we must think of this most beautiful of early buildings.

The tremendous Cantabrian mountains rise in every direction. Oviedo itself is on a steep hillside. The little farms of the Asturianos have granaries raised upon stone pillars, but it is a hundred and fifty miles further, due west, to Santiago de Compostela, and the landscape changes and takes on another character as we descend into Galicia. Lugo, the only town passed upon the way, contains nothing remarkable but its town walls, and I only remember on a previous visit the bull fighters coming out of the hotel – it was a Sunday afternoon – and climbing into an old motorcar on their way to the bull ring. The Gallegan villages give the illusion of standing on hillsides that lead down into the Atlantic, and they have peculiar stone fences that consist of single monoliths set upon edge. Is it only in imagination that we feel we are in the latitudes of Brittany, Cornwall, and the west of Ireland? It is five hundred miles from the Pyrenees to Santiago de Compostela, and the medieval pilgrims accomplished it in thirteen stages. Even now, by motorcar, it is a tiring journey. But the country grows more verdant and laughing; there are villages where the vines are trained right across the street. The churches bear an echo or foretaste of the towers of Compostela and at last, far away, this most holy of pilgrimage centres, second only to Rome and to Jerusalem, comes into sight upon the hillside. It is surprisingly small at a distance, and it is more impressive to arrive there, as I have done on two out of three occasions, late at night.

For in the morning light nothing could be more magnificent than Santiago de Compostela. The first thing one sees, looking out of the window, is a row of statues upon the skyline, and for the lover of architecture there is no greater excitement than to walk for the first time in its colonnaded streets. In this respect Compostela is not inferior to Rome or Venice or to Prague. It is an astonishing experience to find such architecture in so remote a place. It is, even, impossible to make up one's mind to enter the cathedral, there is such glorious architecture on every side. The cathedral, alone, has four distinct façades. And each façade has other superb buildings in the square that fronts it. For instance, the Puerta de Platerías, which will probably be our first point of approach to the cathedral and is the oldest of the entrances, is fronted by a granite building in the local style, known as the Casa del Cabildo. It is of late date (1758) by a local architect, Fernández Sarela, and abstract or expressionist in manner, low, with little windows and a deep balustrade with urns and a kind of abstract, pinnacled trophy or invention based upon the cockle shell of St. James, in the middle. Walking round behind the cathedral, keeping the best till last, the next entrance is the Puerta Santa, and coming round from the back we are in front of the Azabachería, an entrance called after the jet rosaries that were sold there, a façade with steps leading down to it by Ventura Rodríguez, coldest of the Vitruvians, but on this occasion, with his two-storeyed pillared projections, his statues and obelisks, he has emerged into a sunnier clime. In front of this is the immense convent of San Martin Pinario, with a pillared frontispiece in three storeys and a sunken court below it. The golden *retablo*, within, is complicated and over-powering, and deserves Ford's phrase that "it is a fricassee of gilt gingerbread".

But the most splendid building in Santiago de Compostela is the western façade of the cathedral, known as El Obradoiro. It consists of a huge central body in three parts, or it is, in fact, a centre piece with wings, standing on a ramp above a double external staircase that climbs in two flights, with a double row of balusters. This façade is in two storeys, flanked by Corinthian pillars, and forming a huge frame to hold up the statue of St. James. It is an immense gable ending in a cupola, and having first a pair of niches and then one gigantic niche, that hold statues, increasing in size, of the patron saint. It spreads itself, with two lesser gables, across the base of the two towers, two hundred and thirty feet high, all in golden stone, and with snapdragons and other flowers growing in the interstices. The towers, up to their first storey, where they stand on a level with the topmost statue of St. James, are faced with five Doric pilasters on each of their sides, and then climb in two diminishing storeys, ending in a balustrade of obelisks and a high cupola. Seen from below, El Obradoiro is one of the most splendidly fantastic buildings in the world, and except that it is saner and cleanlier it speaks the ecstatic language of the Jain and Hindu temples and could shake its incense-shedding towers above the white-clad crowds and lily tanks of Madura. The architect was a Galician by birth, Fernando Casas y Novoa, trained in Compostela, and the source of his inspiration must remain unknown. In front of El Obradoiro and well below it there lie the Palacio Consistorial, a fine eighteenth century building with an equestrian statue of St. James on its façade, and the Hospital Real, built by Enrique de Egas for the Catholic kings. This, like the Hospital de Santa Cruz at Toledo, was planned by Egas in the form of a cross with four quadrangles and a *retablo* at the intersection so that the patients on both storeys could turn their eyes towards the Host. With its plain golden front, its doorway, its colonnades and splashing fountains, it is one of the most beautiful creations of the Spanish Plateresque.

Enclosed immediately within El Obradoiro is the famous Pórtico de la Gloria, a masterpiece of twelfth century Romanesque, but inferior in beauty to the contemporary French doorways at Moissac and at Vézélay. And the interior of the cathedral of Compostela is French Romanesque, with two storeys of round arches. It is in the style of Toulouse, and of churches at Tours, Limoges, and Conques that were upon the road to Compostela. The high altar of silver, jasper, and alabaster is unworthy of this holy shrine; the treasury was sacked by Soult and Ney, and it is more rewarding to be shown El Botafumeiro, a censer six feet high, over the altar, and so heavy that it is swung from side to side on ropes and pulleys, almost touching the transept ceiling. And to be told that on occasion there is a bagpipe band.[1]

Even now, this is not the end of the wonders of Compostela. There is the extraordinary granite front of the little convent of Santa Clara, built in the middle of the eighteenth century by Simón Rodríguez, another of the local architects, in a style for which a new name must be invented, for it is neither Baroque, Rococo, nor Churrigueresque. The curved motif leading up to the curious hooded roof line, and culminating in a rolled monolith, is as original as any building by Borromini. But El Obradoiro – more than the Pórtico de la Gloria – is the wonder of Compostela. In its towering magnificence it transcends the years of decadence and must be numbered with the great buildings of the world. This remote corner of Spain, so famous as a shrine for pilgrims in the Middle Ages, is still to be ranked with Rome and with Jerusalem.

---

[1] They dance during the processions on the feast of Santiago. And a photograph of the *cabezudos* ("big-heads") grouped together, on that occasion, at an entrance to the cathedral, is reminiscent of the pictures of butter festivals and devil-dances in the lamaseries of Tibet.

2. DANCE OF THE GIGANTONES

*Synagogues of Toledo – Costume of Lagartera – Guadalupe –
Towns of Conquistadores – Plasencia – Charros – Las
Hurdes – La Alberca – Gigantones*

The Prado is an epitome of a quality that is peculiarly Spanish,
the ability to turn a work of art that is extraneous into something that is indissolubly a part of Spain. We have only to
think of what are, probably, the four greatest masterpieces
of the collection in order to realize this truth. They are *Las
Meninas* of Velázquez (now showing like a perpetual miracle
in a room of its own); the Garden of Delights by Hieronymus
Bosch; the Triumph of Death by Bruegel; and the huge Baptism of Christ by El Greco from the Hospital de Afuera at
Toledo. Only one of these paintings is by a Spaniard; the
others are by a Dutchman, a Fleming, and a Cretan. This was
a thought that flashed through the mind passing the Prado,
crossing the Puente de Toledo, leaving Madrid for Estremadura. And it recurred again, less than an hour later, in the little,
bare ugly town of Illescas where no one would think there
was anything worth seeing and where there is one of the most
splendid paintings by El Greco, a St. Ildefonso; and others
of his pictures, too, but this is of the saint sitting writing at
a table, quill in hand, a table four-square as the Escurial, boxed-
in with tablecloth of Spanish velvet. A late painting by El
Greco, closely related to his portrait of the Grand Inquisitor
Don Fernando Niño de Guevara (now in the Metropolitan
in New York) in his horn spectacles and purple silk, a pair of
rings upon each white hand. This and the *St. Ildefonso* of Illescas are the most Spanish of El Greco's paintings; the *St. Ildefonso* for the gold galloon upon the velvet, for his left hand
upon the open book, even for the inkstand and other objects
upon his writing table. The broad gleams of light upon the
velvet are the lights in the sky in El Greco's View of Toledo,
in his Laocoon, in his The Opening of the Fifth Seal.

And coming away, his lurid gleams and flashes obsess one's
mind for many hours upon the road. What is it we read time

and again in Street's *Gothic Architecture in Spain*? – Street who was, on occasion, "sixty-six hours in the diligence with few and short pauses for meals", who dedicates his book to William Ewart Gladstone, and is indispensable, even now. These are his words, "the cathedral is first seen some three or four hours before the city is reached"; and he may continue (of Salamanca!) "the public buildings here are generally grandiose and imposing; but almost all of them are of the period of the Renaissance, and there are no very remarkable examples of this bad age". So he writes; and the trend, now, may be to extol the early and the late buildings to the detriment of the pure Gothic that Street loved. During his "three or four hours" that the cathedral was in sight one had travelled, now, upon good roads, a hundred and fifty miles or so, and at this moment we are, once more, a few miles only from Toledo. There is time to think, while crossing the interminable plain; and I found myself trying to remember El Tránsito and Santa María la Blanca, the two old synagogues in Toledo, for apart from the wooden synagogues in Eastern Poland and the Ukraine these are the only buildings approximating to a Jewish style in architecture, as, also, they are the tangible memorial of the Jews in Spain.

El Tránsito is a great hall, without aisles, with windows in pierced plaster and panels of inscriptions in Hebrew letters; Santa María la Blanca has whitewashed columns with pine cone capitals, horseshoe arches, and arabesques upon the walls. El Tránsito was built in the fourteenth century by Samuel Leví, treasurer to Pedro the Cruel, who was eventually tortured and killed by his master. Both synagogues seem to be haunted by ghosts of the Sephardim; and we can imagine Samuel Leví with his red beard and long gown or caftan, looking like an astrologer, of the same race as the red bearded Nostradamus who was a Spanish Jew of Salon, near Avignon. May not Gil de Silóee, the Jew of Nuremberg, and one of the greatest sculptors of the Middle Ages, have been red bearded too? And we begin to fill the galleries of El Tránsito with Jewesses in their curious and elaborate headdresses and costumes, styles of dress which have not been seen in Spain for four centuries and more, but their traces still exist scattered far and wide with the Sephardim, and in Sarajevo the Sephardim women wore, till lately, a headdress of peculiar shape supposed to be in reminiscence of the sailing ships that took them off from Spain. The beautiful watercolour drawings by Delacroix of the Jewesses of Tangier and of Morocco are well known, and the Jewesses still wear their distinctive dresses in Tetuan, a town which after being entirely destroyed by the Spaniards was rebuilt by Jewish refugees from Portugal after the expulsion of 1492.

But we are a long way from Toledo now. And three hours from Madrid – which in terms of the diligence might have meant a dozen miles, but it is much nearer a hundred – and we are drawing near to Oropesa. The snowclad mountains of the Sierra de Gredos have been long in sight, where the Spanish ibex still hides among the rocks. A little off the high-road a small town appears on a hill above the olive groves. There is an old castle at the summit, and in a few moments we are climbing up through the narrow streets and into a two-storeyed courtyard. It is the Parador of Oropesa, established in the former castle of the Dukes of Frías. The Paradores are another activity of the Dirección General del Turismo; not little modern buildings like the Albergues, but they have been converted from castles or old convents, and serve the same purpose of providing shelter and accommodation, where none is to be had, at important points upon the highroads. The Parador of Oropesa is a convenient stopping place upon the road from Madrid to Seville by way of Mérida, and also for travellers bound for Lisbon via Badajoz. Of modest size, like the Albergues, the Paradores contain a dozen or more bedrooms. They are scrupulously clean, the food is excellent, and the dining-rooms and sitting-rooms are decorated in the local style. The benefits they confer upon the traveller can hardly be exaggerated, and it could be said that the Albergues and Paradores have opened inaccessible parts of Spain to the tourist and made it possible to see some of the most beautiful scenery and architecture in cleanliness and comfort.

There are lovely views from the castle down to the plain

and the distant mountains. And the immediate point of Oropesa lies down there, only a mile away. It is the village of Lagartera, famous all over Spain for its costumes, but it has not yet found its way into the guide books. If it is not a Sunday or a festival there may be little to remark, at first, beyond the knitted stockings of the old women. They are of many colours, and as the female population come out of their houses to stare at the stranger the effect of the stockings is anything else but Spanish. It is more nearly Hungarian in spirit. This could be Mezökövesd. But you have to go into one or more of the houses in order to see the embroideries and old costumes of Lagartera. The whitewashed interiors are spotlessly clean, but without the frantic exaggeration of Volendam or Marken, Dutch villages in which cleanliness has become a bugbear and a nuisance. Being in Castile this is the old Castilian costume, but the broad-brimmed hats and white jerkins of the men nearly disappeared. The women have a richly bordered shawl, worn like a hood, and a multiplicity of skirts and petticoats, each more gorgeously embroidered than the last, one of them, at least, being as red as a tulip and stiffly worked with gold. But it is the embroidery of flowers that is reminiscent of Mezökövesd – that, the short puffed sleeves and coloured stockings. When there is a wedding the dresses are of the utmost magnificence and the bridesmaids in their short skirts are like peasant-ballerinas very much in the model of those of Buják or of Kazár, two other villages in Northern Hungary, near the Slovakian border. It is, in fact, a surprise to see these ballerina dresses worn in Spain, but it is in these short skirts that they dance the *manzana* on the evening of a wedding in the square of Lagartera. This costume is probably a relic of the sixteenth century. At first glance, as we say, it does not look particularly Spanish, still less Moorish, but a book of drawings of Moroccan costumes gives illustrations of a Berber shepherd and of a Berber woman, both of whom present certain and definite analogies with the costume of Lagartera. The first wears a magnificent black goathair burnouse with an orange-red panel of huge and startling size that closely resembles the red tulip skirt of Lagartera. The

99

second wears slippers and leggings that are knitted by the men as they watch their flocks upon the mountains, and that are the exact counterpart of the coloured stockings so quickly noticed in this village. But, costume apart, there is no more to be seen in Lagartera.

Soon after leaving Oropesa we are in the province of Estremadura, bordered all along one side by Portugal, with but few towns or cities: its aromatic hillsides, where the cistus and the peony are in flower, given over to flocks of sheep and herds of pigs; its airs patrolled steadily by the soaring eagle; the crested hoopoe with breast of cinnamon and the black and white barrings of its wings and tail to be seen often by the roadside; the province where Charles V, the Caesar of his age, died in a hermitage; and whence Cortés and Pizarro set forth to conquer Montezuma and the Inca Atahualpa, and to found two new Spains beyond the Atlantic. In many ways it resembles Calabria. The little town of Logrosán, that we pass two or three hours after leaving Oropesa, is built of a black, slaty schist that recalls Lagonegro and the black hills and villages behind Monte Alburno and in the neighbourhood of the vast Carthusian convent of Padúla. That is one of the most Spanish-looking regions of Italy, perhaps in nothing so much as that Calabria, like Estremadura, faces south but has the rugged, bleak hardness of the north. Calabria leads to Naples and the Campagna Felice, to Italian song and trellised vines; Estremadura to Seville, to the bull fight and the *seguidilla*.

But Estremadura is the province of the rockrose. It is blooming in every direction and the sides of the road are like a flowering garden: the white cistus, chiefly, with its chocolate or maroon-red blotches; but there are the crimson and purplish rockroses, as satiny of texture as the white, with beautiful cup-shaped flowers. These have been for centuries the winter feeding grounds of the merino sheep, which go back in summer to León and Castile. It is a country that is famous, also, for its hams; and traversing Estremadura I wondered from what part of the province came those particular *jamones*, mentioned by Ford and other travellers, that are cured from pigs that have been fed on vipers. These "viper-fed" hams, cured in the snow of the sierra, are described a hundred years ago as being obtainable in London, and it was satisfying, therefore, to see one exposed for sale in 1939 in the window of the same emporium in Piccadilly and to be told, on enquiry, that these were indeed the hams of long ago which were suddenly in supply again after a lapse of "many years".

The valleys grow narrower and narrower, and the swine-herds and their black charges block the road. In these villages the whole street is often absolutely illumined by the beautiful plumage of the cocks and hens. I have never known a country where the barn door rooster is so magnificent in colour. There are game cocks which may well be descendants of fighting cocks brought into Spain by Wellington's officers. I noticed several Blood-Wing Pyles (a fighting breed with blood-red markings said to have been a favourite with our Charles II);[1] but also, in Estremadura, there are a strange breed to be seen with scraggy necks, as though existing in a state of per-petual nervous and mental preparation for the table. The wooded valleys grow narrower and damper; there are ferns and mosses and damp exhalations. The road climbs, and sud-denly we see an enormous group of buildings, the size of the Papal Palace at Avignon, rising out of the hillside about a quarter of a mile away on the spot where the shepherd found the statue of the Virgin. I have been twice to Guadalupe, and both times it has been in pouring rain. The place is associated in my mind with the sound of rain falling in courtyards, with long, cold passages, and steamy heat. For after a time it stops raining and the sun comes out. But I remember best the rain splashing on a palm tree and the monastery garage which is nothing other than a huge and disused Renaissance church. The monastery is occupied by monks (Franciscans) and the sensation of staying a night there, feeding in the guest room, drinking the red wine, smoking and talking round the *brasero* with Padre Victorino, the monk-musician who is organist, and

[1] Upon the hill of the Albaicín, at Granada. The "naked-necked" fowls are reported from Hungary and Transylvania, but I can find no previous mention of them in Spain.

going along the endless passages to bed, is as though there were still monks at Alcobaça or Batalha. In the morning we áre shown the monastery. We see the two-storeyed cloister with its Moorish arches, the Mudéjar brick fountain or *glorieta* in the middle, the Camarín with its decayed paintings by Luca Giordano, the Sacristía and its eight pictures by Zurbarán the Estremaduran master, and the collection of vestments second only to those in the cathedral at Toledo. But the most beautiful memories of Guadalupe were sitting beside Padre Victorino in the organ loft while he played a *saeta*, a reminiscence of Holy Week in Seville, with drum and trumpet sounding magically from the far end of the church; and looking down from the balcony of my bedroom over the pigs and chickens of the houses, far below, to the little triangular *plaza* with its arcades and wooden balconies, so like other Spanish village *plazas*, so like the *plazas* of Candelario or La Alberca.

It is more beautiful, still, to be on the hillsides among the rockroses, with a soaring eagle seen against the rocky mountain opposite, and to pass, as we may do here, a tattered family of Gypsies. But the country becomes more wild and savage as we near Trujillo. It was only in Trujillo, I must state in parenthesis, that we saw thin and famished-looking persons in 1947, and children who were hungry. The town resembles a steep cone of decaying masonry. In the Plaza Mayor there are a fine Renaissance palace and the so-called "home of Pizarro"; and we set forth, climbing in search of his tomb and of the house where he was born. We came, first, upon the latter, a little roofless cyclopean hovel with an enormous round arched doorway; and in the church of Santa María de la Concepción we struck matches and found the kneeling figure of a knight in stone. This is the tomb of Pizarro, to whose lot fell some of the most extraordinary adventures that have ever befallen man. He was the son of a swineherd. But in the Temple of the Sun at Cuzco he saw the twelve golden lifesize statues of the Incas and the Inca's garden planted with golden fruits and flowers. And having ourselves seen Trujillo and the secular misery in which he was born it becomes easier to understand the spirit of the Conquistadores. His descendant, after more than four centuries, the Marquesa de la Conquista, still has a "palace" in Trujillo with a corner balcony of the Renaissance, splendid heraldry above, and estates in the neighbourhood.

Cáceres, the other town of the conquerors of Mexico and Peru, is thirty miles away, defended, we would almost say, by a multitude of little rocky mounds. It has many *casas solariegas*, town manor houses more than palaces of the Conquistadores, with doors of granite and splendid coats-of-arms. The churches are many and disappointing, and there is a little granite Templete or Arco de la Estrella by Churriguera, revealing the "heresiarch" in tame and urbane mood. Upon the façade of one old house may be seen the coat-of-arms of the Montezumas, with the sun in the middle. There are still Spanish families who bear this name. We stayed the night outside Cáceres, not knowing where we were going, and came to a villa or small country house in the process of being turned into a kind of country club. There were *tir-aux-pigeons*, swimming pool, tennis courts, all in embryo, even a miniature racecourse and a mechanical organ, while, outside in the golden light, a couple of peacocks were displaying. It was, at the same time, peculiar but lonely, for we were the only guests. Half-past nine approached, a charcoal *brasero* was put under the table (an old Castilian custom), and we enjoyed one of the most excellent dinners I have ever eaten. Ford, and we are left to imagine what this means, says the inn or *posada* at Cáceres, in his time, was "very bad". The reflection that the villa belonged to a relation of the Marquesa de la Conquista, to some one, therefore, in whose veins there flowed, in diminution, the blood of the Peruvian Incas, lent a deeper romance to the singing of the nightingales.

We now continue south, though we have to cover the same road again, to Mérida. This city was the Roman capital of Lusitania (Portugal) and it still has Roman remains of the first magnitude: the gaunt silhouettes of several aqueducts with piers eighty or ninety feet high which are the playground of the storks, a superb bridge across the Guadiana, a theatre and an amphitheatre. A town bathed in an almost Andalucian

103

sunlight, with whitewashed houses, and boasting a Parador with a pretty flower garden established in an old convent. Badajoz is forty miles to the west and I am sorry not to have seen it, for this town on the frontier of Portugal has a Gothic cathedral with pictures by Zurbarán and by the other native painter Luis Morales (El Divino), the author of so many Madonnas with high, egg-shaped foreheads. It is from the country between Mérida and Badajoz that the "viper-fed" hams may have their origin, for the road passes within sight of the Sierra de las Víboras, "infested by numerous vipers which are eaten by the pigs and said to swarm with snakes and reptiles of every kind". However that may be, nothing could be more magnificently wild than the landscape working north again from Mérida. A country of bare outlines, and with the mountains and the plain expressed with an intensity and an economy of means that must remind all who have ever admired them of the early etchings of *Les Saltimbanques* by Picasso, in which the group of horses and men from a roadside encampment holding them are "put into" the plain and against the mountains in just the simplicity of means. These are not yet the white plains of Andalucía, nor the white houses and the bridge seen through a great arch of *Le Tricorne*, an imaginary and poetic Andalucía that we must place nearer to the Mediterranean. But, making to the north again, we could see in the distance great grazing herds of *toros bravos*, the stork was nesting in every village, and soon after passing a little town with the imposing name of Garrovillas de Alconetar we crossed the Tagus.

It was a Sunday morning when we stopped at the foot of the steep stairs leading up, like a short cut, to the cathedral of Plasencia. This is the most fortunate of entrances, for from the terrace at the top, overlooking the river, you have the best view of the octagonal "beehive" dome of the chapter house, another of the Périgourdin or Salamantine domes that are so Oriental in appearance. It is a ribbed dome, though "dome" is a misleading word for a high and conical building more resembling a Seljuk *tekké* at Konia or Adalia, and it has little circular turrets at the corners. The west door is a four-storeyed

Renaissance frontispiece, not unlike a Tudor mantelpiece, and the cathedral, as a whole, shows the handiwork of Rodrigo Gil de Hontañón and of Juan de Alava, architects of the New Cathedral and of San Esteban at Salamanca. The interior, probably because it was never completed, gives an inordinate impression of great height and an undisturbed feeling of centuries dead and gone. It is in this spirit that we must enter the *coro* and look at the seventy-two choir stalls which form one of the most extraordinary relics of the Middle Ages. The sculptor was a Southern German, calling himself Rodrigo Alemán, and he worked in two manners, in flat "line", where his "drawing" recalls early woodcuts by Dürer, if those could be seen raised in low relief, beautiful in detail, especially in the hands, the faces, and the hair; and in the round, where Rodrigo Alemán shows himself in pornographic vein and on the underneaths of the seats, when lifted up, often gives a parody or caricature of the religious scene immediately above. Among subjects that can be named are a lady occupying a bathtub with a friar; but the whole *sillería* argues a great force of personality on the part of the sculptor who must have been at work for many years in some sort of a shed or workshop attached to the cathedral, and have had his handiwork continually under observation by both priests and public. His carvings are best described as a huge volume of double drawings illustrating religion and reality, occupying the working hours of half a lifetime, and having seen them we would wish to know more of this contemporary and remote disciple of Dr. Faustus in a far-off Spanish town. It is no surprise to be told a legend that the sculptor, having stated that God himself could do no better work, was imprisoned in one of the towers of the cathedral. (It has none.) He lived there on the birds he was able to snare and with their feathers made himself a pair of wings. With these he threw himself from the window and was dashed to pieces on the ground. This is an old story that would please no one more than Rodrigo Alemán, and he must not be grudged the degree of immortality that he would have wished.

North of Plasencia the landscape becomes more mountainous, and still continuing upon the Sunday morning the pretty

105

country town of Béjar came into sight, and upon the far side of it a wonderful cattle fair was being held upon the hillside. There were great rings of black bulls. Countrymen, dressed in their best, with the long sticks of cattle drovers in their hands, were hurrying towards it. We could see booths and music, and the green hill was black with bulls and peasant. A few miles further on we passed the signpost, but the signpost only, of a road leading to Montehermoso. This village is as famous for its costume as Lagartera, and on the Sunday morning we could have seen the costumes. Like Lagartera, it is not mentioned in the guide books. They are, nevertheless, perhaps the most beautiful of all the Spanish costumes. The chief feature at Montehermoso is a most extraordinary hat. A straw hat with a wide brim and an immense tip-tilted crown, a high crown that tilts so far forward that it presses down, almost, upon the brim, but the straw is, in fact, nearly concealed with embroidered bands and by feathers and rosettes of brightly coloured wool. In effect it is a straw bonnet that leans forward and that nods with flowers. Underneath this the women wear a flowered silk kerchief folded on their heads with its fringed ends trailing down upon their shoulders. The old ladies wear a "skeleton" edition of this straw hat, bearing the same relation to it that the "skeleton" clocks standing with all their works exposed under a glass dome bear to the ordinary old clocks. Just the straw shape, that is to say, and with a sort of open floral fence of straw work round the crown. Some of the young women wear a corner of the silk kerchief round their mouths covering their necks, or they bring forward both ends of it and hang them on their chests.

They wear embroidered shoulder capes reaching to the elbow, long sleeves, cuffs heavy with embroidery, and accordion-pleated skirts, calf-length, with white stockings and black shoes. They have aprons, the length of their skirts, and beautiful flowered silk ribbons, a pair of lace bands between, making four ribbons in all, of equal length, that hang down from their waists behind. These skirts, which can be seen on market-day in Plasencia when the country people drive in from Montehermoso, are of every colour. They may wear four, six, or even eight pleated underskirts, the pleats all fitting exactly; in green, in reddish-purple or fuchsia, in yellow, light blue, or wine-coloured, the purpose of such colours, it is evident, being to make an effect of the utmost brilliance when dancing; and we are given a photograph of a young girl of Montehermoso sitting with her back to us upon a straw chair. She has lifted up and folded back one of her underskirts with its borders of different colours and it forms a huge hemicycle behind her, while she puts one of her hands in its wide cuff upon her knee, and looks round at us under that flowering brim with the fringed ends of her kerchief falling upon her shoulder. There seems to be no clue as to the date or origin of this curious and delightful costume, which was worn formerly, as well, at the nearby Malpartida de Plasencia. Surely it is not enough to say that the straw bonnet and the silhouette suggest fashionable dresses of the eighteen-thirties? On the contrary, some authorities have put forward the theory that traces of the Montehermosan costume are to be seen among the Indians in certain villages in Bolivia and Peru, whither they could have been taken in the time of the Conquistadores. Certainly, some of the Indian costumes show the influence of sixteenth century Spain, and I have seen photographs of Bolivian Indian women, especially, wearing hats and costumes resembling those of Montehermoso.

Nearer still to Béjar – it is but a couple of miles away – there is another centre of local costume at Candelario, remarkable for the flowered black velvet *mantillas* worn by the women when they go to church, over an elaborate kerchief that frames in the face, and for their short capes or jackets of yellow or green velvet. But the province of Salamanca, to which we are now returning, is the region of the *charros* and the *charras*, who dance to the music of the *dulzaina* and the *tamboril*, peasant farmers in white linen shirts, stiff *sombreros*, short jackets, and tight trousers, their women in bell-shaped skirts of dark green or purple and velvet capes covered with much gold embroidery, bits of glass, and long streamers of ribbon, the prototypes – more in name than fact, for the style has much altered in the ages – of the Mexican *charro* horsemen in their huge sombreros, gorgeous jackets, glittering harness

107

and great saddles, a costume which is dying out in Mexico in spite of some attempt made to preserve it. The purest type of *charra* costume in all Spain is said to be that worn at Aldeadávila, on the Douro, and only the width of that river from Portugal. *Mantillas* of black velvet are worn, and golden filigree ornaments upon the hair. Another beautiful *charra* costume is that of Palencia de Negrilla, in the province of Salamanca. A nobleman of Spanish descent, Don Carlos Rincón Gallardo, Marqués de Guadalupe, y Duque de Regla, is leader of the Mexican *charro* movement. This old gentleman was to be seen in Mexico City, riding in his beautiful costume with a *charro* attendant following, and he had even adapted a black *charro* dress with silver ornaments for evening wear. A certain village in Mexico, Amojoc, an hour from Puebla, is famous for the *charro* clothes and saddlery that are made there. The Duke died in 1950.

If Lagartera and Montehermoso, together with the unique and extraordinary La Alberca which we shall explore shortly, have the Spanish costumes with most character, there are others near Segovia that are scarcely less typical of Spain. At Zamarramala, on the feast day of the saint, the *alcalde* and the *alcaldesa* (mayor and mayoress) wear long black cloaks and a dress of velvet with gold panels that can be guessed, at first glance, to date from the reign of Philip IV. At Amblés, near Ávila, the women wear loose kerchiefs and straw hats adorned with flowers and feathers, bits of glass, and long streamers. Other villages, Turégano, Sepúlveda, Pedraza, were the sources of Zuloaga's early and best paintings: men in black sombreros, black breeches, capes and jackets, in the rocky landscapes of Old Castile. There remain a few types more that should be mentioned. The dresses of Ibiza, smallest and most primitive of the Balearic Islands, a fishwife's costume of shawls and many golden necklaces; but in one small village, San Antonio, there is a peculiar costume suggested, it is said, by the paintings in the pulpit of the village church. It consists, for men and women alike, of a wide hat and slashed jacket of early seventeenth-century Breton type; but, also, it suggests Spanish Quakers, if such existed, who have been stranded on a coral atoll. The Mallorquinas have distinct and charming dresses of flowered silk, with a silk shawl framing their faces and falling stiffly to their elbows, a shawl worn like a headcape so that the upper part of their body is concealed in it. With this they wear a fan-shaped starched ornament just below their chins. The bagpipe players, again, in their broad-brimmed hats and baggy breeches (*bragon bras*) are counterparts of those of Brittany. Nowhere in the Balearics, although it might have been expected, is there any likeness to the wonderful Sardinian costumes. If those resemble anything Spanish it is the costumes of Aragon. A certain authority sees in these bagpipe players a suggestion of the *gauchos* of the Argentine pampas, but here we cannot follow him, for there is no trace of the red that was the *gauchos'* favourite colour.

One of the most charming of all Spanish costumes is worn at Puebla de Guzmán in the province of Huelva, inland from Huelva, and along the frontier with Portugal. It is an Amazon costume worn by women members of the *cofradía* when they ride on horseback to the shrine of the Virgen de la Peña, and consists of a full reddish-purple velvet skirt with gold embroidery at the hems, a white shirt worked with a sprigged pattern and a top hat! A white lace veil falls from the back of the top hat to the shoulders, and the top hat has an ostrich feather worn like a cockade in front. It seems hardly possible that this dress has not been affected by French riding fashions of the eighteen-thirties, but it must be a spectacle of enchantment to see a few ladies, thus attired, riding to the Romería. It is one more to be added to the Amazon costumes that we described at the Feria. And we would end, for like so many of the others this is a costume that could have an effect on modern fashions, with the *magas* of the Canary Islands, another race of equestrienne altogether, for in fact they ride upon camels. The *magas* of Tenerife wear a delightful little round straw hat perched on one side of their heads; they, also, favour huge flopping straw hats in the summer, while the *magos* (camel drivers) wear white baggy kneebreeches, a black cummerbund, and a long white woollen shepherd's cloak, and it is thus that the oranges and bananas of the island are brought down to market.

There has been time enough to think of Spanish costumes as we drive along over the endless plateau, but at length the hills slope down towards a river, and not much more than a dozen miles from the frontier with Portugal we see the roofs and towers of a town. It is Ciudad Rodrigo, as famous in the Peninsular War as Badajoz, but not a third the size, and once it must have been as often on the lips of Englishmen as El Alamein. A small, dull market town, with fine walls and a goodish cathedral with nice cloisters; but the approaching traveller will be forgiven for feeling some apprehension as to his hotel. The truth, in the case of Ciudad Rodrigo, is of the nature of a delusion, for as you drive through the town and the streets grow narrower you come out, at last, in front of a low, containing curtain wall, with nothing visible beyond it, and continuing, find yourself at the doorstep of the Parador of Henry II, installed in an old castle of the sixteenth century in midst of the town walls, with wonderful views over the river towards Portugal, and offering every possible combination of cleanliness and comfort. Here we rested three days and collected newspapers and letters. It was a curious sensation to be staying in this remote place, but the third day, having seen the sights of the town, we resolved late in the afternoon, never having heard of it before, on a visit to La Alberca.

Between Béjar and Ciudad Rodrigo there lies the famous wild district of Las Hurdes, a name deriving from an old Basque word which means a pig. All sorts of legends are current in Spain about Las Hurdes, and to listen to these it would seem that the inhabitants are mentally and physically afflicted, like the population, a generation or two ago, of some of the Alpine valleys above Aosta. Of those it used to be said that one in fifty was a cretin and above half more or less goitred. In the Valais scarcely a woman was free from it and those who had no swelling were laughed at and called "goose-necked". Some had tumours as large as their heads appended to their throats and, I am quoting from a book of 1874, "there are instances in which the increase is so enormous that the individual, unable to support his burden, crawls along the ground under it". Somewhat of this nature were the stories prevalent about Las Hurdes. Until recently there were no schools there, and I remember the interest in the newspaper some years ago when Don Alfonso rode through it for three days. There was said to be a large proportion of dwarfs among the population and that inbreeding had produced many idiots and imbeciles. Some friends who went through Las Hurdes recently by motor (showing there are roads) could confirm none of these stories, though they said that inside the wretched houses the sensation was that of finding yourself in a peasant's cabin of five hundred years ago. They saw one or two half-idiots, but their impression was of the sturdiness of the people and of the wild loneliness of the country. In this latter respect there can be nothing in Europe to equal Las Hurdes, this side of sub-Carpathian Russia. The district consists of three parallel valleys and several villages on the slopes of the Sierra de Gata, not far from another valley, that of Las Batuecas, where there used to be a famous monastery, long ago burnt down, "with a lofty wall about three miles in circumference enclosing gardens and groves, the surrounding eminences, covered with fine timber, being studded with hermitages", so says Ford.

La Alberca, to which we are now setting forth, lies on the other slopes of the Sierra de Gata, less than ten miles from Las Batuecas. It is excitingly near, therefore, to Las Hurdes. An afternoon that threatened rain, but the wind was too boisterous in that great, open country for the rain to fall. Two elements added further excitement: there were no signposts and we had scarcely any petrol. La Alberca *should* be eighteen or twenty miles from Ciudad Rodrigo, but there was no hope of a petrol pump and not a living soul in sight to ask the way. At last there was a village, but no one knew the distance to La Alberca; they could only calculate two hours or so, by horse and cart, which might mean anything from six to ten miles, or more. And some way from this village the road forked, and there was no possible indication as to which fork to take. Neither road was metalled; neither had telephone poles along its side. There was nothing to distinguish one road from the other, and little more than a gallon showed on the petrol gauge. But the road we chose by instinct began to climb into the olive groves. Soon there were great orchards of apple trees to either side, and we must be in the zone of cultivation of some village or small town. There were ancient walnut and chestnut trees. It was raining gently; and we reached the first houses and the road came to an end.

There is no wheeled traffic of any sort in La Alberca. You can only go into the town on horse or mule back, or on foot. And La Alberca is decidedly a town and not a village, for there must be between two and three thousand persons living there. It is, as certainly, the most extraordinary centre of human habitation in which I have ever set foot. The streets or alleys, which are at the same time open drains, are strewn with enormous stones or boulders in lieu of pavement, and you have to pick your way. Ford, the only English author so far as I know to mention La Alberca, describes it as "a dingy hamlet composed of prison-like houses built of granite". Even in his day, a hundred years ago, the "hamlet" had little short of two thousand inhabitants. But he is speaking half-truths. Black they are, indeed, but the Stygian, Tartarean alleys are lit up with the flaming colours of the cocks and hens. The ground floors of the houses are of granite, with smaller stones above that, but their overhanging upper storeys are of great baulks of timber. It is difficult to indicate the degree of darkness of the side alleys, but already one dreads the thought of La Alberca after nightfall. Those wooden upper storeys, upon a bigger scale, are like nothing else but Berber villages. And now we have come out into the *plaza*, where the houses are for the most part whitewashed, with wooden balconies. All round the *plaza* the ground floor is an arcade of granite columns. There is a granite church standing among more open drains, with fiery cocks and hens disputing for what they can find between the cobblestones.

But, after all, is the population of La Alberca who are the greatest curiosity. A number of them sat or stood about under the granite columns. There were old peasants in black kneebreeches and waistcoats, for this was an ordinary week-day; but on feast days there are still remnants of what was

112

once the richest and most beautiful costume in the whole of Spain. It is in this costume, moreover, that there may be discovered the clue to the inhabitants of La Alberca. It is not so particularized in the case of the men, although they wore the widest-brimmed sombreros of the whole kingdom, sombreros with flopping brims only equalled in size by those of the Chod clansmen of the Böhmer Wald, near Domazlice, who guarded of old, the Bohemian frontier with Bavaria. But it is the women's costume of La Alberca that yields the Berber or Mudéjar origin. Unfortunately, it was so valuable for its gold and silver ornaments that it used to be divided at every death in a family and can only with difficulty be assembled again.

The dress, itself, is of heavy velvet with much gold galloon. But the headdress is of white lace or gauze with silk ribbons sewn into it, worn low down over the eyes, and entirely covering the mouth and chin. The other feature is the extraordinary array of necklaces falling as far as the knees, and formed of row after row of enormous gold or coral beads, with rosaries, amulets, reliquaries, and ex-votos, all worn over a sort of golden apron. The characteristics of the costume are the Berber headdress and the enormous necklaces. These were bought from the *charro* jewellers of Salamanca who worked, within living memory, upon these Berber ornaments of the twelfth and thirteenth centuries. The book of coloured drawings of Moroccan costumes to which I have referred on p. 99 gives instance after instance of this profusion of necklaces worn by the Berber women, and the analogies are too obvious to need stressing. Particularly, the *tehlil*, a little silver box containing a verse from the Koran, might have been removed from one of the necklaces of La Alberca. and we must compare, as well, the heavy necklaces of the Maragatos, to whom, also, a Berber origin has been ascribed. La Alberca, to those who could withstand its rigours, must be a wonderful storehouse of folklore and of legend. Of the extent to which these, or its music, have been studied, I am ignorant, but this large rural population must be the most conservative in Spain. I do not know if there are Berber words in its dialect, but certainly the origin of its inhabitants is not that of the population of the rest of Spain. They are a race apart, like the Maragatos. Finally, the women of La Alberca are extraordinarily reminiscent of that masterpiece of sculpture, the "Dama de Elche", one of the sole relics of Iberian art in Spain.

How does it come about that these descendants of the Berbers, the Mudéjares or Moriscos, have been isolated here in this remote corner, in the next valley to Las Batuecas and Las Hurdes? But there is contained in those words both the question and the answer. Coming away from La Alberca – running away, if you prefer it, for the dread was ever-present of finding ourselves without petrol and having to stay the night there – we arrived at another of the crossroads and, as before, could not decide which way to go. The truth is that this region along the frontier of Portugal, and both sides of that, is one of the remotest parts of Europe. Perhaps the costumes of Puebla de Guzmán, of Montehermoso, of La Alberca, of the Maragatos are a proof of that, for all of these are strung from end to end along that frontier. But we came down through the orchards and the olive groves, out of the walnut and the chestnut trees, over some miles of plain, with our last drops of petrol to Ciudad Rodrigo, a frontier fortress like Badajoz, guarding, we could testify, a curious and forgotten stretch of land.

Looking from a window, before dinner in the castle-Parador, more than ever like a fortress now that we had returned to its safe shelter from La Alberca, a wild rain was sweeping over the huge open plain towards Portugal. It blew and shook the windows, it rattled at the doors. This keep or bastion in the town walls stood out into the wild weather with such an isolation that you felt you were on a ship at sea, and by an easy altering of the focus of the eyes could imagine that the castle itself was moving. The sensation, too, a little resembled that of a long siege, and while looking at the map, waiting about in the rain wondering whether or not to go to La Alberca, we had been told by the manager how difficult it was to provision the Parador – fish had to be brought all the way from the sea via Madrid, meat from Salamanca, and so forth, and there was little but eggs and chickens to be had from nearby –

114

all of which added to the delusory effect of good food, central heating, and hot water, in so distant and remote a place. The extraordinary village we had seen that afternoon, and all these different but contingent circumstances, must have excited my imagination, for all night long, more often awake than sleeping, my mind was full of visions of the tremendous Spanish cathedrals and churches, those which I had seen already and those that I still hope to see, for these loaded shells of architecture and the unparalleled treasures that they hold can become nearly an obsession to anyone who loves Spain. I lay thinking of Cuenca and of Sigüenza; Cuenca, a hundred miles and more from Madrid, out in the middle of New Castile, with only of late years a railway beyond it down to the Mediterranean at Valencia, a town on a rock, like Toledo, Ronda, Segovia, Ávila, with a wonderful old cathedral[1] and eight bridges over its two rivers, a town I had always wanted to visit because of my absorbing interest in the Carlist Wars.

For it was Cuenca that was taken and sacked in 1874, during the second Carlist War, by order of Doña María de las Nieves, the wife of Don Alfonso Carlos, the brother of the Pretender. I have written, elsewhere, of my memory, as a child in Venice, of seeing Don Carlos stepping into his gondola from the Palazzo Loredan, of his rowers in scarlet liveries, and little negro page. Don Carlos died in 1909, and his brother Don Alfonso Carlos became Pretender to the Spanish throne. Many years later an Austrian friend of mine, who lived near Don Alfonso Carlos at Ebenzweier, described to me his memories of meeting Don Alfonso riding with his wife Doña María de las Nieves. Two horsemen in liveries of scarlet and gold, the colours of Spain, preceded them. Then came Don Alfonso Carlos, in a tall top hat, wearing long black trousers and golden spurs, mounted on a black horse; while Doña María de las Nieves rode a snow-white charger by his side. When they walked together their negress, "Frau Poppetta", went respectfully behind them. All this, and more besides, I put into a book which another friend sent to Don Alfonso Carlos, and

[1] The most splendid *rejas* (wrought iron grilles) in Spain are to be found in the cathedrals of Toledo, Seville, Burgos, and Cuenca.

115

the old gentleman replied, on notepaper bearing the arms of Anjou and Spain, for he was titular King of France as well as Spain, and saying that he would have written to me personally, but that he could not do so as I had spoken of him as Pretender, not as Claimant, to the Spanish throne. Meanwhile, the memoirs of his wife, *Mis Memorias*, had appeared in print in 1934, sixty years after the events described.[1] The old lady, eldest of the six beautiful daughters of Dom Miguel, the Portuguese Pretender, wrote this astonishing military compilation in the style, exactly, of an old soldier. Many battles, including the taking of Cuenca, are given in full detail. She was not twenty years of age at the outbreak of the second Carlist War, but proceeded at once to Spain and distinguished herself in command of her husband's army. The Carlist armies were divided into regiments of Basques and Zouaves. Doña María de las Nieves shared the hardships of the field with her troops and appeared, daily, on horseback, on her white charger. At the siege and taking of Cuenca, as elsewhere, she wore uniform, and sported a kind of Zouave jacket lined with astrakhan. Her tunic was covered with medals, she carried a gilt riding switch, and her headdress was a bright red Basque beret or *boina* with a long gilded tassel.

And tossing uneasily in my thoughts, while the wind still howled and roared outside, I would turn from Cuenca to Sigüenza. The beautiful effigy of the *Doncel*, the young knight who was killed at the taking of Granada, is in the cathedral at Sigüenza. It is a building that, according to report, has more even than its due share of sculpture, including a sacristy with a barrel-vaulted ceiling carved with three hundred, or another authority says three thousand, heads in high relief, all different, and indeed it would have been more difficult and painful still to have made all three thousand or three hundred heads the same. But, more interesting, during certain festivals the choristers at Sigüenza wear pages' dresses, like the Seises of Seville cathedral. Do they, too, we wonder, dance with castanets at

---

[1] Dona María de las Nieves was eighty-two when the first volume of her memoirs appeared. Don Alfonso Carlos died in Vienna in 1941, and she survived him till 1943.

the high altar? This is on eight days during Corpus Christi; on the afternoons of eight days for the Immaculate Conception; and for three days during Carnival, a total of nineteen performances, yearly. It is supposed to be a survival from the Mozarabic ritual, Seises meaning "six", but there are, more often, eight or ten small boys. They are dressed, at Seville, like pages of the reign of Philip III (1598–1621): "crimson doublets with yellow stripes, and white satin kneebreeches slashed on the outside to show a crimson and yellow lining; their stockings are white, and they have white shoes with crimson and yellow laces. Over the right shoulder they wear a white sash, ending in a crimson and yellow tassel on the left side." Their hats are of damask to match their tunics, turned up in front to show the white satin lining, and with a plume of coloured feathers at one side. They wear their plumed hats while dancing, and are attended by a man in black, wearing a wig and a white ruff, and carrying a silver mace. But, at Seville, they wear scarlet and white for Corpus and blue and white for the festivals of the Virgin.

Sigüenza is upon the borders of Old Castile and Aragon. And as I lay, trying to sleep, I travelled in imagination a hundred miles further, over the Ebro to Barbastro. For a particular reason. The cathedral at Barbastro has great columns springing into fan-vaulting, as in Perpendicular England, the only instance of this fanciful and extreme invention outside the British Islands.[1] How the Mudéjar craftsmen would have loved this fantasy, and what might it not have come to at the hands of Juan Güas! And I arrived in my dream at Sariñena, between Lérida and Zaragoza, passing on the way "an enormous deserted Cartuja (1732) on a hill, with a huge church, cloisters with many chapels, and vast dependencies", in order to visit the convent of Sigena. This was one of the casualties of the Spanish Civil War, and like the palace of the Infantado at Guadalajara it is a total loss. It was a royal foundation of the twelfth century; there were kings and princesses buried there, and many tombs of abbesses and noble ladies.

[1] Barbastro is another of the Spanish towns where there is religious dancing during the processions at Corpus Christi.

117

There is, or was, the most tremendous of round arched or hooded Romanesque portals, a stone doorway with some fifteen concentric ribs or mouldings. But the interest of the convent at Sigena is that it was the sole surviving relic of the Knights Templars. They were nuns of the Order of St. John of Jerusalem, the only ones of their kind, and we have come to admire their dresses. They could be seen at mass in the choir or walking in the cloister. For they wore the clothes of ladies of the twelfth century, of the time of Don Alfonso II of Aragon and Doña Sancha of Castile. They had long veils or wimples and headdresses of fantastic and enormous size. They wore the red floreated cross of the order upon their left breasts, but these enormous headdresses, as we shall see, were only for special occasions. According to an old authority on the monastic orders there were sixty nuns, who lived by day in separate apartments but slept together at night in a vast *dortoir* or dormitory, and the abbess, following the custom of Doña Blanca, daughter of Jaime II of Aragon (d. 1336), had a court about her of seven nuns who were always with her. There was the *Custode*, who received strangers, did the honours, and attended to the private affairs of the abbess; the *Camarera*, who served her in her chamber; a cupbearer, who gave her to drink; a *Repostera*,[1] or keeper of the wine cellar; and others who served her at table and looked after her person; and the abbesses of Sigena were always attended by this court in miniature. Divine service was performed with much pomp and majesty; and upon such occasions the nuns wore *rochets* of fine linen and held a silver sceptre in their hands. It may have been only the abbess, and not the nuns of high degree, who carried the silver wands or sceptres in their hands, but those persons who penetrated to this remote convent and saw the particular headdresses of the nuns, worn until 1935, have testified to their extraordinary complexity and elaboration, being the headdresses of royal princesses of the early fourteenth

[1] The Reposteiro Mór (officier du palais attaché au garde-meuble) was among the Grandes charges de la Cour at the Court of Portugal, according to an old almanack for 1857, also a Meirinho Mór (Grand-Huissier), and a Porteiro Mór.

118

century, requiring an immense patience in the making and rivalling in complexity with the sixty or eighty pins necessary
for the hair of Princess Aurora in *The Sleeping Beauty*, for
her vermilion hair when she runs from the colonnade into
the garden, and makes her entrance in her bodice and short
tutu of silver and cloth-of-roses. . . .

I must have fallen asleep at about this moment, though I
seemed still to have in my ears the roaring and buffeting of
the wind, but to this there quickly succeeded a drumming and
beating of another kind. A drumming of the sort that suggests a spectacle or attraction in a public fair; "something",
whatever it is, walking with the drummer, or that the curtains
of a booth will be quickly pulled aside. . . . There are sinister
figures, too, among the crowd, personages, as in a dream,
out of one's own memories or mythology; taking the form
of a little dwarf who is waiting at a railway station. To be
exact, at Catania, in Sicily. He is waiting in order to lead us
to the churches and the convents; to San Benedetto, where
the dormitories are six hundred feet in length, so long that they
finish in a point of light: to the Palazzo Biscari with its fantastic staircase balustrade. And there is the cretin or idiot
of Cefalù. . . . The evil little figure of a man in a straw hat, with
a quick step, who walked by my side in my dream, and taunted
me in the School Yard at Eton. . . . And suddenly, bordering
the road, the wall falls back a little and gives a breathing space.
Beside the gate pillars, on separate pedestals, stand two statues – one of a Chinaman and the other portraying a pierrot –
with more affinity to the vegetable than the human world.
His head is like the flower sheaf of an arum lily, his ruff like a
bundle of reed flutes, and the rest of his body more of a
flower stalk than a human trunk and legs. He and his companion
are markedly of a night world, carved with the ragged and
deep relief that looks best by starlight. This is the threshold
of the wizard world of Prince Palagonia. . . . The idiot of Toledo, too, who lived down in the town of shacks, below the bridge
of Alcántara, when I first went to Toledo in 1919; who had
a horrid trick in which he gnawed his arm, the short, stiff arms,
held close to his side, of the typical mattoid; carrying a short,

knobbed stick, and wearing a beret on his head. . . . And I distinctly recognized the terrible dwarf Juan II, whom I had got to know from the illustrations to M. Legendre's *Las Hurdes*, 1927, before leaving London for Seville: a barefoot dwarf with curving limbs, a horrible round face, and wearing a curious travesty of a fisherman's sou'wester, just such an inhabitant as one would have expected and imagined for Las Hurdes.

But the drumming gets louder and louder, so that it is making towards us, and we find ourselves under the walls of a cathedral, we do not know where, and we must walk round another corner in order to find out what it is. But this takes us out of all human proportion. We are in the land of Gog and Magog. What we see is a terrifying and enormous giant. And another and another. It is the dance of the *Gigantones de Tarasca*. A huge and terrible giantess, hatless, and with a fixed smile or grin, dancing in a doorway. She has curling hair, parted in the centre, great earrings, and a fearful shawl or blanket on her arm. We see behind her, on the wall of the church, the knotted cable denoting the *orden tercera de San Francisco*. Her companion wears the black cape and long cloak of a night watchman or *sereno*. He has a round Spanish hat and holds a long stave in his wooden hand. He too is smiling, and as he dances we notice how small and disproportionate are his feet. In front of them, and half their size, stands the man who plays the pipe and drum.

But now, with the inconsequence of a dream, we are close to a great cathedral doorway with row after row of carved stone figures standing in niches under canopies. The cathedral door is open wide, and outlined against the black depths of the interior, nearly the height of the entire doorway, stands an enormous pair of giants, a Moorish man and woman. These are less frightening in appearance. In front of them, a man on horseback, in feathered hat and ruff, in position as though he has ridden out through the cathedral door, has two attendants in red, dressed like the *chulos* of the bull ring. But the freaks and giants are of two dimensions. And there is a lesser order still. These are the "big-heads", the *Cabezudos*. They are all grouped together under the stone figures of the portal.

120

A man in a cocked hat, staff in hand, like a beadle or town crier; next to him a dolt or zany; a young woman with a huge face, powdered white, wearing a flowered dress; a hideous Filipino in a sailor's jacket and straw hat. Beyond him, to the left hand of the doorway, a "big-head" in a velvet hat, with side whiskers; at the back, a Moorish page in a white turban, but of intermediate size, half-way between the giants and "big-heads"; and then, more "big-heads", three or four young women wearing shawls or bonnets; a negress housewife; ending with a "big-head" in white wig and *tricorne*, lace cravat, and flowered eighteenth-century clothes.

And moving, in the nightmare, into another corner, we behold a far older and more gigantic tribe of giants. They are standing in a row, with wooden arms straight down their sides. A King and Queen in crown and ermine robe, who must be meant for Ferdinand and Isabella, and are as old as the king and queen upon a pack of cards. A Moor in a turban; an African king; a Chinaman; a lady with fine hair and features, the more horrible for her gigantic height; next to her, a man with Roman features and a Red Indian feathered head-dress (we have had Africa, Asia, Europe, this must be intended for America); and last, a perfectly gigantic woman wearing a ribbed jacket, huge necklace, long sleeves, and nightmare, tattered skirt.

Who are they? What can they be? For they come forward tottering and shaking, lifting their feet from side to side, dancing to the pipe and drum. The King and Queen in crown and ermine dance a slow measure, but cannot lift or move their arms. The Moor and the negro king dance together. But the rest of the giants stand in a line. Their turn has not come yet, and all the children of the town are at their feet, a number of small boys dressed like pages in white stockings and round caps, and others who wear dunces' caps or the paper mitres of boy-bishops. These are hardly higher than the giants' knees. The *Gigantones* must be sixteen or eighteen feet in height. Now, the horrible, fat laughing woman and her night-watch-man come tottering forward. They are *Gigantillos*, eight or nine feet high; but no living giant was ever so fat as that, or

121

large of feature. And the "big-heads", the *Cabezudos,* are but a head taller than a man. . . .

Edmondo de Amicis is describing his visit to Toledo cathedral.[1] He, and his guide, went from the cloister towards the bell tower. "When we had climbed half-way up, we stopped to take breath. The guide knocked at a little door, and a little sacristan appeared and opened another door leading into a corridor, where I saw a group of gigantic puppets most curiously dressed. Four of them, so the guide told me, represented Europe, Asia, America, and Africa, and two others, Faith and Religion. They were made so that a man could conceal himself in them and raise them from the ground. "They are taken out", added the sacristan, "on royal fête-days, and carried about the city." Then, wishing to show me the *modus operandi,* he got under the petticoats of Asia. Next, he led me to a corner where there was an enormous monster which, touched at some point, extended a very long neck and a horrible head, with deafening noise. He could not tell me, he said, what that horrible creature meant, and begged me to admire, instead, the marvellous Spanish imagination, which created *so many new things* that it could furnish them to all the known world. I admired, paid, and continued the ascent of the bell tower.

Whether these curious figures are still housed in Toledo cathedral, I do not know. They may have been destroyed or burnt during the Civil War. When I saw them in 1919 they were not, as described by Edmondo de Amicis, in a room in the tower, but in the Claustro Alto, or upper cloisters. There were Europe, Asia, America, and Africa, and the dragon Tarasca; also, a figure of the Cid and a comic giantess called Ana Bolena. The whole collection were known as the *Gigantones de Tarasca.* They were carried through the streets at Corpus Christi, and I remember seeing the procession waiting to start outside the south door or *puerta de los Leones.* Ana Bolena seemed to be the most popular of the giants and giantesses. But there are, or were, these figures in other places

[1] *Spain and the Spaniards,* by Edmondo de Amicis, translated from the Italian by W. W. Cady, Putnam's, 1881, pp. 244, 245.

besides Toledo. A number of them were at Burgos. The figures of Ferdinand and Isabella, of the fat woman and the night watchman, who appeared in my nightmare, were at Burgos. The two last, as I have said, were *los Gigantillos*, the others were *los Gigantes*. The "big-heads" or *Cabezudos* came from Tarragona. At Pamplona, according to Ford, "the tutelar of the town is San Fermín, whose grand holiday is on the 7th of July; then *los Gigantes* (images representing Moors, Normans, etc.) visit the town hall, dance before the cathedral, and pay their respects to their patron's image at San Lorenzo." At Pamplona, on this occasion, bulls are let loose in the open streets. It is one of the most astonishing spectacles to be seen in Spain. The public join in, and one or two of the casualties are often fatal.

So there are, or were, figures of giants at Pamplona, Burgos, and Toledo. No doubt there are more in other places.[1] All of the figures may not be old in themselves. They may have been renewed at later dates. The "big-heads", *Cabezudos* of Tarragona, look as though they could not be older than the second half of the last century. Others, Ana Bolena, Ferdinand and Isabella, the Four Continents, are much earlier, and may date from the end of the seventeenth century. But it is difficult to tell. They are so early in idea. They belong to the world of moving figures upon clocks. We have already seen the hour struck at Astorga by the Maragato and Maragata;[2] but the most celebrated inhabitants of this sub-world must be the pair of giants in bronze who strike the hour with their hammers on the clock tower in the Piazza of St. Mark. There are far older clocks with moving figures in English

[1] And in other countries. In the treasury of the cathedral at Metz there is to be seen the "graouly", or dragon, which was formerly taken in procession through the city streets. During the fiesta of the Virgen del Pilar at Zaragoza on 12 October there are processions of *Gigantes* and *Cabezudos* through the streets. These puppets are kept at other times in the old Gothic Lonja or exchange.

[2] When at Astorga, I failed to notice a weathercock on the cathedral tower, which, says Ford, "is the statue of Pedro Mato, a celebrated Maragato, carved in wood, and painted and modelled in the peculiar costume of his clan".

cathedrals; one, of the fourteenth century, at Exeter, and a clock at Wells which was made by a monk of Glastonbury about 1325. All of these, and there are so many others, have, to greater or lesser degree, the clockwork, waxwork horror attaching to them, which is the same as that pertaining to ventriloquists' dummies and all puppets, even to the carved face on the jester's staff. Their appeal is to rudimentary sense of humour and to a population that cannot read or write. It is our Lord Mayor's Show in primitive condition.

And this gives the clue to their date. The *Gigantones de Tarasca* are of the "period" of *Dick Whittington*. They are of the kin of *Mother Goose* and *Jack and the Beanstalk*. Spain, where so much of the past is still living, may be the only country in Europe in which these "big-heads" and dummies are still part of the cathedral establishment, and are still carried in procession. To have experienced that dream, having known them long ago at Corpus Christi in Toledo, was no matter for surprise, having seen, so lately, the choir stalls of Rodrigo Alemán and the tapestries of Zamora, and having been, that very afternoon, to La Alberca. . . . Ana Bolena tottered forth to dance, the dragon Tarasca roared and shook his head; and it could have been the wind howling, or the ghosts of old battles in the breach of Ciudad Rodrigo.

3. ARAGON

The Doncel – Calatayud – Zaragoza – Small Towns of Aragon

Spain is, of all countries, that in which to apprehend the music of high-sounding names. That there is meaning behind their proud syllables, who would deny! We will take a town at random, Madrigal de las Altas Torres, the forgotten village that was the birthplace of Isabel la Católica.[1] It is a name that no one with the spark of poetry in him is likely ever to forget. Tarragona, Tortosa, Teruel, there are a thousand or ten thousand

[1] The brick ramparts of Madrigal de las Altas Torres form an exact circle 744 yards in diameter. It is an example of the military art of the Mudéjares.

17   Cuenca, in Castile

18 The lovers of Lagartera

19 Santiago de Compostela: façade of El Obradoiro, 1738

21   Salamanca: costume of La Alberca

20   Segovia cathedral: the crossing (1563-91)

22   Catalonia: mountain landscape

23   Segovia: Roman aqueduct

24   Salamanca: Charras from Palencia de Negrilla

more; Tarazona, Barbastro, Cuenca, it is a list which could be continued for ever, but which it is not necessary for our purposes to carry further than the prime divisions of Castile and Aragon. What perfect balance or opposition there is between their parts! What an independence of sound while they were separate; and what harmony after the marriage, when they were united and became one!

Of the towns of High Castile I have attempted to give some account already, but, now it has been my opportunity to go for the first time to Aragon, and this chapter opens at Medinaceli, which is precisely upon the borders of Aragon and Castile. Being Spain, it would be but normal to anticipate some difference in the landscape and architecture of the two kingdoms, and it is the purpose of this chapter to set forth in what these contrasts and differences consist. But, first, it is necessary to recapitulate that coming away from Madrid the road passes through Alcalá de Henares, half an hour from the capital, where Catherine of Aragon and Cervantes first saw the light of day, where there is one of the finest Plateresco façades in Spain, that of the university, by Rodrigo Gil de Hontanón, with heraldic centrepiece, figures in relief, and window *rejas,* but a town, in short, that is the Spanish garrison town *in excelsis,* where every Spaniard has had a relative at some time or other in the army, and of which the military life and the cavalry bugle calls are made immortal in *les Dragons d'Alcalá* of *Carmen.* Guadalajara is the next town on the road, with the melancholy ruin of the Infantado palace, a disaster and a shattering of poetry so complete and entire that it is more inspiring to read the names of Brihuega and of Pastrana upon the signposts; the first of these a little hunting château of Carlos III, now a cloth mill, but with its garden carefully preserved (or so it was some twenty years ago). It is a hanging garden raised on a terrace, with green arches and obelisks, with memories of Caserta, a garden Beckford would have loved, and that by some magical distillation of memory brings one near to Tiepolo, of whom Carlos III was patron, and a garden, above all, in which it is impossible not to be reminded of the extraordinary strains of music to which that king must have been accustomed in his youth, when the eunuch Farinelli was singer and Domenico Scarlatti was harpsichord master and composer. Pastrana has associations of another character altogether. The small church had, rolled up on the floor of the sacristy, the splendid Gothic tapestries of the conquest of Arzila in Morocco by Alfonso V of Portugal (*El Africano*) in 1471, tapestries which had to be trodden upon as they were unrolled, of Tournai manufacture, not inferior to the finest of those at Zamora or at Zaragoza. They had been given by Felipe II to his mistress, the Princess of Éboli, who bequeathed them to Pastrana. The tapestries are no longer at Pastrana; they were sold some years ago, but I had seen them hanging from nails and trailing their fading colours on the dusty floor.

And the road from Madrid to Zaragoza had this other attraction, that it passed near to Sigüenza, one of the smaller towns that I had never visited and wanted most to see. The secondary road leading there plunged in bold curves into a deep ravine, and having come up the other side led out into infinity over the rolling hills, and no sign of Sigüenza. When it, at last, appeared it was a little town on a small hillside. The cathedral is a Romanesque building under Cistercian, that is to say, Burgundian influence, with a beautiful rose window, a wealth of stucco portals and wall decorations in what Mr. Bernard Bevan calls a hybrid "Mudéjar-Florentine Renaissance" style, and many early paintings including some panels of the Umbrian school. But the tomb of the *Doncel*, Don Martín Vázquez de Arce, the young knight killed by the Moors before Granada, is a disappointment. His features are hard and lacking in poetry. I could have wished I had not seen it. But the *Doncel* had his father sleep through eternity in their chapel in that place of beauty, and if there be such a thing as the communion of dead spirits they have much to talk of.

It is at Medinaceli, or soon after, that we enter Aragon. No need to be told that this little village with the proud name is upon a Roman site, for there is a Roman arch visible from far below. The road winds up to it, and into the yellow sunset, and when you arrive there is nothing more than a church, a few old houses, and a white Albergue. Nothing could be deader than Medinaceli. An old man, slippered like Pantaloon, comes creeping from a building the size of a palace and shuffles across the draughty *plaza* to unlock the church, which is enormous and empty, but has fourteen coffins of the Medinaceli family. There is nothing more in the village, which is as cold and draughty as an empty stage. But the view from the Albergue is magnificent beyond description. Far below runs the river Jalón, but we look over miles and miles of treeless, scorched tablelands and distant mountains. And descending into the valley are soon in Aragon, at a point where a reddish tinge comes over the landscape and a stratum of chalk comes to the surface, giving the effect of a diurnal moonlight, as of the chalky, powdery moonbeams in the red light of day. Now comes Ariza, a little town with a ruined castle and many cave dwellings of the Spanish troglodytes scooped out of the chalk, haunted, it should be, by the ghosts of earlier inhabitants, for they have been lived in for many centuries.

But all of this region, entering Aragon, is full of cave dwellings. The road passes a round, flat-topped hill of yellow clay, and all the seam just under its flat surface is worked and dug round into caves. Some are walled up with loose stones and are used for granaries, but in the doorways of others there are women standing with their babies, and children are climbing up the steep and stony slope, and they are lost to sight just as we are thinking of their curious lives under the crust of the earth's surface. But now the distant hills are white as snow and barren as dead bones. And the immediate Aragonese foreground is of an intense bloodless red, as though powdered with a rusty or ferruginous dust. This is the typical Aragon, and it is entirely different from Castile, as different, indeed, as their two names. Even the villages are of baked mud with the fleckings of the straw. It is an Africa without palm trees, closely resembling such Moroccan landscapes as that around Ksar es Souk. And Aragon has been the land of the Mudéjares. It would appear that the majority of the population in medieval times was Muhammadan. Many tens of thousands of Mudéjares were driven away in the sixteenth century, yet, in Mr. Bernard Bevan's words, "the Moriscos, as they were called after their forcible conversion, were still so numerous that the number of those expelled from Aragon in 1610 amounted to sixty-four thousand", a half, or more than half, in all probability, of the rural population of that Kingdom. The Mudéjares were skilled workmen, and have left their mark in Aragon in the tall brick church towers of the fifteenth and sixteenth centuries, which they built for their Christian masters, but which belong more to Moslem than to Christian art. The first of the hexagonal brick belfries, or church minarets, is to be seen at Ateca, a town in the midst of vineyards. It is completely Oriental in appearance, giving expectation that these octagonal towers are a chapter missing from the histories of Moslem art.

And we come to Calatayud, one of the principal towns in Aragon, announcing itself beforehand with its Mudéjar but Christian minarets, and steep hills behind, which are honeycombed with caves. It is not for nothing that the winding way up to the ruins of the Moorish castle, among the cave dwellings, is called the Morería. But Calatayud is more ancient of history than the caves or brick towers of the Mudéjares. It is but two miles from Bilbilis, an old Iberian town that was famed for its goldsmiths and armourers, its iron mines and horsefairs, and as the birthplace of the poet Martial, of whom Ford remarks that "although an Aragonese by birth, he was in truth rather an *Andaluz gracioso*. He went to Rome, to the court of Domitian, where he neglected business, and took to writing epigrams and *seguidillas* in the style of his countrymen Salas and Quevedo." But his fellow Spaniard Trajan neglected him, and Martial came back to live near Bilbilis, and to die. By now, we are in the deep narrow streets of Calatayud, which many opinions would agree are more Oriental than those of Toledo or Granada. There are *paseos* and *alamedas*, too, and we can look up at the tall brick towers. Their octagons are ornamented in brickwork by setting forward some of the bricks, with herringbone patterns and intersecting arches, and in the result the towers of Calatayud are as Oriental as anything in Fez or Cairo, in Delhi or in Isfahan. One of the churches, Santo Domingo, long destroyed, had a polygonal apse with external Moorish patternings, horseshoe ornaments, and frieze of stalactites, all in brick, and must have been among the most curious of all Christian buildings. The still existing Colegiata de Santa María, which began duty as a mosque, has a richly figured portal of the Renaissance under an overhanging porch of tiled woodwork, an *alero* as they are known in Aragon, but they correspond exactly to the projecting porches of the *madrasas* at Fez and at Marrâkesh. This church has one of the most imposing of the Mudéjar belfries. Within, the *coro* has run riot, and the Churrigueresque stuccowork includes figures of lifesize winged horses reared up on their hind legs above whole enfilades and perspectives of Salomonic columns in black marble. The same architect of sculptor worked here who carried out the stucco carvings and revetments to the chapels in La Seo at Zaragoza. The church of San Andrés has another of the octagonal brick towers. And there is another Colegiata, that of Santo Sepulcro, with a domed lantern and a pair of towers, though later, not Mudéjar, in origin. The towers of Calatayud, in the steep light of midday, in all weathers and at all times of day or night, in the teeth of the *Moncayo* and in the rain showers, but most, it may be, when the electric lights are shining in anachronism from the open doors of the cave dwellings along the Morería and the Camino de la Soledad are of the Orient, indubitably, and as much so as if they had the actual form of a pagoda or of a minaret.

Between Calatayud and Zaragoza, passing a village famous for its peaches, and more villages with the octagonal Mudéjar towers, every few moments we are once more among the troglodytes. There are cave dwellings cut into the rock out of conical red hills; and at another place, houses hollowed out of a seam of chalk with only their chimneys emerging, or, it could be said, lowered into the chalk up to tops of their chimneys, and no more showing. Further on this road, but we did not see it, at Epila, there is a castle of the Dukes of Híjar, with cave dwellings at the back that, we were told particularly, form one of the beauties of the place and that are hung with chintzes and coloured cotton stuffs for wedding days or other celebrations, for as at the Albaicín of Granada there are rich troglodytes and to live in a cave does not denote poverty. But

129

the domes and towers of Zaragoza are seen from afar, and half an hour later we are in the capital of Aragon.

Two long streets, lined with shops selling religious medals and emblems, lead down to the Ebro and to the two cathedrals of El Pilar and La Seo. El Pilar may be one of the most sacred shrines in Christendom, but it is lacking in anything other than an emotional importance. The frescoes by Goya are bad and early, not to be told apart from those by Bayeu and others of his contemporaries and elders. Even the alabaster *retablo* by Damián Forment, and the one hundred and fifteen stalls carved in oak in three rows, by a Florentine, are lost in the tawdry environment and have no value. Perhaps the prettiest things in El Pilar, the pearls and diamonds apart, are the vestments of the canons, tied up in neat bundles in the sacristy, bound with red or green silk ribbons to match their colours, and worked with the initials of their reverend owners. But El Pilar, as we shall know, is not the only church in Zaragoza that has a touch of the boudoir or the drawingroom.

The co-cathedral of La Seo, by contrast, is of entire magnificence, glorious in decay, though tawdry in its parts. The exterior is insignificant, without façade or frontispiece, to be entered, always, by stealth, as though going into it by the wrong door. It has an octagonal tower, "drawn out into four divisions or stages like a telescope", says Ford, and built by an Italian. Within all is Spanish magnificence and ornament run riot. The innumerable chapels have proscenium arches – they could be called nothing else – as wide and high as the prosceniums of many theatres, but surrendered to a delirium of ornament. If they were gilded, and not white stucco, they would be as rich as anything in Mexico. We recognize, here, the same hand that worked at Calatayud. The *retablo* of the altar is of alabaster, as complicated in Gothic detail as those of Burgos and of Seville; the *sillería* has stalls for an archbishop and sixty-eight clergy; the *trascoro* is unsurpassed in richness with so many carved scenes and figures that they weary, and you fain would pass them by. And from the very midst of this wall of carving, opposite the main door, there projects a *templete* of six black, twisted Salomonic pillars supporting a baldaquin on curving volutes, "marking the spot where the Cristo de la Seo", or according to another account, the Virgin, "spoke to Canon Funes", whoever Canon Funes may have been! In such a church as this it is essential to look in the sacristy to see what treasures it may contain, and the sacristies of La Seo consist of an enfilade of grand apartments, the end one furnished like a drawing-room with long pier glasses and great vases of Chinese porcelain set upon the floor. Perhaps the only thing lacking is a China mandarin to nod his head and lift and let fall his outstretched hands.

There had been a catafalque, that evening, before the high altar, in the light of many candles, with a priest's biretta laid at the head of it, the funeral of "un sacerdote" of La Seo, we were told, and in the morning when we came to see the tapestries we found them closed until his funeral mass was over. In this manner we witnessed one of the most inspiring religious ceremonies that I have ever seen. It has certain points, moreover, which may be peculiar to the old cathedral of Zaragoza. The singing was beautiful, of the Italian operatic sort, now seldom heard, music by a composer to whom I could not put a name, a Spaniard of the early nineteenth century, no doubt, and contemporary of Eslava. But it was the procession that was so curious and moving and that took one so entirely out of the present world into an age that one had thought was, long ago, but dust and mouldering bones. I must explain that, the night before, when leaving La Seo, I had caught sight in the deepening gloom of a man dressed like a notary or lawyer's clerk of the mid-eighteenth century, and wearing a short, close fitting wig, close and unkempt, or ragged from long wear, and to which his face and the expression of his features had, as can happen, grown into or accustomed themselves. He was one of the two beadles of La Seo, and they may be the only pair of living persons who have worn wigs, day in, day out, for fifty years. Both beadles, in their wigs, now appeared, leading the procession.

There were priests and canons in every shade of purple and scarlet, of violet and crimson, and they now proceeded to make the entire circuit of La Seo, a progress which was the more theatrical and thrilling for the spectators because the *coro* of a Spanish cathedral takes up its whole central space, so that you could hear the music of their chanting muffled in the distance, and could come forward and post yourself at the far corner of the *coro*, where you heard and saw the procession advancing toward you, looming larger and louder at every step. For it is necessary to get that low note into our account of this funereal progress. First came the pair of beadles in their yellow, musty wigs. Then the files of priests and canons. But an extraordinary feature was the group of choristers, with a choir master to beat time for them, who walked leaning his free hand upon the head of one or other of the choir children, while, immediately behind them, came a man in a frock coat holding a brass instrument, a trombone or bass clarionet, upon which, every now and then, he blew a low, rumbling note. The visual image was that of a man in a frock coat blowing a conch or seashell, until you caught the brass glitter of the instrument and the telescope movement of the piston valves. The purpose, of course, was to give the note to the men singers, and the echo of that long, low note shuddered and died against the Gothic vaults of the cathedral. At a moment when the whole procession was hidden behind the *coro* it blew again, and once more, and now the identity of this peculiar and extraordinary effect yielded up its secret. For I had heard it before. I knew its long, low, shuddering emptiness. It is an effect made by Berlioz in certain moments of his *Grande Messe des Morts*. It is described as one of his "experiments", intended to give the "impression" of the echo of a brass instrument dying away in some immense cathedral, but no one who heard and saw this funeral procession in La Seo can doubt that, like so many more of his strokes of genius, this was inspired by something that he had heard in youth. I cannot think otherwise than that Berlioz must have heard this very effect in childhood in some village church in his native Dauphiné where the sexton and gravedigger, both posts in one, blew, as well, the "serpent". Or it may have been in the churches of Lyon or of Grenoble; but wherever and when it was, during the French Empire and the wars of

Napoleon, though a custom old in its day, even then, and dating from and earlier age. Each time the low note was blown, in La Seo, in image it was like the opening of the charnel house; not the general gaol delivery, not the bursting of the prison bars, but the note or signal for the unlocking of the key, the drawing of the bolt, the breaking of the leaden seal. A note blown by a devil, not an angel, if one has to believe in such things; and at the mock day of Judgement staged by an anti-Christ before he is interrupted by the real One. But the procession came into sight again round the corner of the *coro*. First, the beadles in their wigs, the scriveners, the attorneys, the écrivains, or I would call them, in parody, the Writers to the Signet, stage lawyers who know no law at all; and then the bishops in violet, the *penitenciario*, the *canónigos*, and minor priests and canons. And the "serpent" in their midst rumbling its low note of warning. Again and again it sounded. The procession came past in front of us on its last turn of the cathedral. The man in the frock coat lifted the "serpent" to his lips; the shuddering, forlorn note died back against the ceiling. Yet once more; and the beadles in their wigs and the bishops in violet robes disappeared into the archway leading to the sacristies. But the chanting and the "serpent" note continued, and we followed them. They were gathered round a folding baldaquin on six posts that stood upon the sacristy floor, and we stayed there for some moments among the pier glasses and the tall china vases, until the man in the frock coat blew the last note on the "serpent" and the chanting ended. It was of a curious significance to hear the singing and the trumpet note of the procession, which had seemed out of this world altogether and dwelling in a fortified or sanctified past of their own, now sounding within the four walls of this ecclesiastical drawingroom. But it was over and done, and the last notes died away.

After this wonderful Spanish church ceremony, and the violent appeal of its mournful magnificence to the imagination, it was nothing exceptional to be led by a sacristan along a high corridor, up a splendid staircase and into the museum of tapestries. This is formed from the sets of tapestries belonging to both cathedrals, El Pilar and La Seo, put together, and it is a sensation of a marvellous order to set foot within these rooms, hung with the most beautiful fabrics of the Middle Ages. Close to the door of the first room there is the famous tapestry of *Las Naves,* or the Expedition of Brutus, nephew of Aeneas, to Aquitaine, and at the top is inscribed in Gothic lettering that the armada was composed of nine galleons, well equipped, carrying soldiers, horses and engines of war, passing the Pillars of Hercules for the coasts of Aquitaine, which, we are to understand, means the mouth of the Loire. The tapestry is of French, i.e. Arras, not Tournai, weaving, and this panel is the middle hanging of a set of three, the others not being in existence. To the right we see the armada at sea, or rather, coming into shore, and to the left the battle and the disembarkation. At the left foot of the tapestry there stands a group of personages, intended for Brutus superintending the arrival of his galleons, and in the rendering of his flowered robes of dark green velvet or brocade the weavers have surpassed themselves. But it is the medieval ships that are the unique beauty of this tapestry. The nine galleons are there, filling the entire foreground with their "packing case" forms and their masts and rigging. They are like the ships upon the golden "angels" of Edward III, rising high out of the sea, with balustraded poops, and crowded with persons. At least one horse is on board, in obedience to the inscription in the weaving. To the left, and but a foot or two from Brutus upon the shore, there is a galleon with ladies on board in tall steeple hats, and a pair of heralds are blowing into their trumpets, which have long pennons attached and which look like dragons' wings, and at first glance might be mistaken for ships' rudders because of the way they lean forwards and downwards and dip into the waves. Another galleon, nearer still, right in the foreground of the tapestry, has a man climbing into the rigging, a lady on board in velvet and brocade with a steeple hat of extreme and fanciful elaboration, and a herald who holds his trumpet away from his lips, waiting for the order, and the pennon and the trumpet mouth touch the waves. But the battle on shore is too complicated to follow. There are knights in full armour riding their battle chargers, and a giant foot soldier, sword in hand, in the attitude of an executioner, as in a beheading of St. John the Baptist, with his back turned to us, and the bodies of his victims lying at his feet.

Upon the opposite wall to this marvellous work of medieval art there hangs a beautiful tapestry, one of a Brussels series of the Virtues and Vices, early sixteenth century in date, which is a little late for Gothic tapestries. This panel has for subject Original Sin and the Passions in the life of man; all the principal human passions, vanity, avarice, ambition, luxury, appear with their appropriate emblems, there is a quite extraordinary amount of liturgical and symbolic detail, and the designer of the cartoons can only have been an authority himself on Catholic law or dogma, or must, at least, have worked in close association with persons learned in religious law. This tapestry in beautiful tones of blue and red, and in the multitude of wild flowers strewn upon the spring-flowering meadows, must have attained to entire technical perfection in the art of tapestry weaving, and it could only be compared in this respect to the finest of the Persian hunting carpets. Perhaps, to some tastes, this tapestry is a little "full blown", portending that the art has reached maturity and passed its youth. Another great tapestry is a Crucifixion, beautiful beyond description as a hanging, but earlier and rougher in weave, by that much the more appealing as a work of art. In other and further rooms, hung with tapestries along their walls and on long screens, there are unforgettable details that stay in the memory: a group of young ladies in a room in a high tower wearing the most complete "collection" of steeple hats that could be imagined; a man on the wall opposite with a fur hat, and in the same tapestry a man in a striped cap, like a chef's cap but "carried out" in tones of blue and red. The Museo de Tapices of Zaragoza is one of the glories of Spain, and the French or Flemish tapestries have become as Spanish as the paintings of Hieronymus Bosch from the Escorial or the Moorish arches of the mosque at Córdoba.

The Mudéjar leaning tower that was the sensation of Zaragoza, and that was the probable masterpiece of Mudéjar building, has long since been pulled down. This octagon, the Torre Nueva, as high as the Giralda (300 ft.), was "rushed up" in fifteen months, proving the proficiency in tower building to which the Mudéjares had attained, under the supervision of two Mudéjares and a Jew. It ended, under its cupola, in curious Tudor-like brick battlements, and must have presented an extraordinary spectacle leaning ten feet out of the perpendicular above the roofs of the old houses, a minaret falling, falling, falling on the Christians below. One or two old palaces still remain in Zaragoza; and there is the Aljafería, now a barracks, with coffered ceilings, brick arches and traceries as "Oriental" as anything in Delhi or Agra, and with an unlikely identity as being the setting for part of Verdi's *Trovatore*. But we return to the brick octagonal towers of the Mudéjares, for they require further treatment as one of the sights peculiar to Aragon.

There are instances in which the octagonal tower rises from a square base, but the most original feature in the Mudéjar towers, and one which has not been mentioned, is in their use of colour. At Utebo, the Campanar de los Espejos is tiled in floral patterns of green, blue, and golden yellow on a white ground. This is, decidedly, a building to which might be applied the phrase of Fergusson (speaking of San Pablo in Zaragoza) that "it might pass for a church in the Crimea or the steppes of Tartary". This was completed in 1544, in the reign of our Henry VIII, and two generations after the Moors, in popular opinion, had been "driven out" of Spain. The "belfry of the mirrors", as its nickname could be translated from the Spanish, is every bit as curious as the Church of St. Basil in the Red Square at Moscow. There are, as well, the octagonal *cimborrios*, or lanterns, of La Seo, in Zaragoza itself, and of the cathedral at Tarazona, which is in three stages or storeys.

But the outstanding use of colour by the Mudéjares is, or was, at Teruel, a town in Aragon half-way between Zaragoza and Valencia, to be reached by way of Calatayud with the Moorish towers, and beyond this point I can draw no further upon personal experience, but must write from hearsay. At Teruel, according to Mr. Bernard Bevan, there were nine parish churches, one in the centre of the town, and eight beside the walls, as a result of which, in four cases, there are streets running through archways in the towers. Of the towers that survived until the Civil War, two, according to the same authority, were the glories of Mudéjar art. "Both towers", he says, "were clothed in Muslim robes, . . . the windows being divided by terracotta colonnettes, scarlet, green, and turquoise. In both towers – San Martín and San Salvador – green and white disks were inset . . . the cathedral tower had purple and olive green colonnettes; San Salvador had a roof of white and apple-green tiles; while other churches had tiles of canary-yellow and cobalt blue." San Salvador, we say in parenthesis, had a Churrigueresque interior and an Indian-sounding miraculous image, *El Cristo de las tres manos*. But Teruel must have been dazzlingly, theatrically picturesque, with as many towers as Calatayud, coloured, not plain brick, and giving the illusion, therefore, that they were minarets.[1] Our view of the town from a high parapet along its walls shows San Salvador to the right, the Torre san Martín in the middle, and to the left the twin towers and dome of Santiago. What are missing in the drawing are the green-topped tower of San Miguel, which, in fact, was formerly a minaret, and the sharply pointed green *cimborrio* of the cathedral. The green-tiled minarets and domes are reminiscent of Morocco.

Twenty miles from Teruel is the picturesque small town of Albarracín. This is an extraordinary huddle of flat roofs under a mountain which is scaled and surrounded by Moorish walls and towers. The town stands on a ridge encircled by a river, and a great stairway ascends to it from out the valley. It has a cathedral and other churches with Mudéjar towers, and an Ayuntamiento supported on the hillside by giant brick buttresses. Ford writes of Albarracín that "the pinewoods provide fuel for numerous ferrerias or smithies, in which the abundant iron ores are rudely smelted as in the days of the Celtiberians. The air is scented far and wide with the perfume of wild flowers. The honey is delicious, and Moya, with the hills near the Gabriel, is the Hymettus of Spain; from hence

[1] Teruel was much damaged in the Civil War.

137

probably came the *mel excellente hispanicum* which is lauded by Petronius Arbiter." In another direction from Teruel lies the secluded Rincón de Ademuz, belonging to Valencia, but only in communication with Teruel, a small mountain town untouched since the Middle Ages, and with an altarpiece by the Valencian primitive Reixach, in whose name the curious-minded may like to trace a Jewish origin.

The buildings of the Mudéjares in Aragon have left towns like Calatayud and Teruel more Oriental than European of aspect, and their octagonal church towers and *cimborrios* are features as peculiar to the Christian idiom as are the churches with painted exteriors in the Bucovina. Probably it is only because the traveller usually passes through Castile on his way from the French frontier to Madrid that the character of Spain is deduced from Castile only, and not from Castile and Aragon. But we return to our hypothetical journey and arrive at Alcañiz. This lies in a different direction, down to Ebro from Zaragoza, in the olive groves below the mountains. A huge castle stands on a hill above the river, and the Iglesia Mayor has a white Rococo façade with a recessed portal and a roof line rising in steps, like gables, with urns or vases on its stages.

But, after Calatayud and Teruel, the most beautiful of the towns of Aragon must be Tarazona. This is up the Ebro from Zaragoza, a little way into the mountains beyond Tudela, in the corner of Aragon next to Navarre. Tarazona, heralded by the poetry implicit in its very name, is another of the theatrically, romantically picturesque towns of Spain. The cathedral has a brick cloister, which once had cut stone Mudéjar traceries, "not intended for glazing, but an ingenious arrangement for rendering the cloister cool and unaffected by the sun", and a lantern or *cimborrio*, already referred to, of which Street remarks that "such a curious and complex combination of pinnacles and turrets built of brick, and largely inlaid with green, blue, and white tiles, is perhaps nowhere else to be seen". It must be the prospect of Tarazona that most pleases, and in the drawing we are walking below the huge Palacio Episcopal, like the palace of some lama or living incarnation, raised upon brick arches, with many windows and balconies, with the roofs of the town cascading down below it, and the high brick Mudéjar tower of La Magdalena piercing the sky of Aragon.

But we leave Zaragoza for the last time upon an imaginary excursion and it takes us to Huesca, the capital of a province and half-way to the Pyrenees. The cathedral has a *retablo* in alabaster by Damián Forment, sculptor of the *retablo* in El Pilar at Zaragoza. His subject is the Passion, and it is a triptych with elaborate frame and pinnacled canopies, and *predelle* underneath. In Spain, the land of *retablos*, this is one of the most rich and beautiful works of its kind, comparing with the masterpiece of Gil de Silóee in the Cartuja de Miraflores outside Burgos. It is difficult to believe that a town so far to the north of Spain as Huesca was a Moorish stronghold, but the cathedral is on the site of a Moorish mosque. The smaller town of Jaca lies much further into the mountains, into the full white circus of the Pyrenees. This walled city with twenty-eight towers and seven gateways has an early cathedral, too, and in June, upon the anniversary of a battle with the Moors, the young unmarried girls of Jaca go through the motions of a mock battle in memory of the bravery of their ancestresses against the Moors. Here, too, during the festival ceremonies inside the cathedral they dance a *jota*, to the music of two bagpipes and a *tamboril*.

But an account of Aragon must close with some mention of the mountain village of Ansó, which is celebrated for its costumes. This is one of the villages, like Montehermoso or Lagartera, that is not even indexed in the guide books. The inhabitants of Ansó are famous gardeners, noted for their growing of vegetables and medicinal herbs (which they sell in other parts of Spain), and the skirts of the women are best described as being of a lettuce green. One account says that they resemble gigantic heads of lettuce. They are bell-shaped, very full skirts with long plaits and folds, of a light green baize woven locally, and the headdress consists of nun-like draperies with an ornament like a phylactery hanging upon the forehead. They spin the white linen of their collars and puffed sleeves.[1] A whole row of women of Ansó kneeling in their church betrays the Oriental origin of these draperies, for the headdresses are Moorish, not medieval Spanish in effect. The dress of the men of Ansó is uninteresting, except for their violet *fajas* (belts). It is only the women who are peculiar and beautiful in their green skirts, and who are Oriental, also, in their movements, and still more in repose, as when kneeling in church or sitting outside their house doors in the steep and cobbled streets.

[1] Ansó lies near the secluded valley of Roncal, in Navarre, wherein there are seven village communities of which the mayors wear fine white linen ruffs resembling Walloon collars.

3

Valencia and Levante

1. BARCELONA, TARRAGONA

To Catalonia – Barcelona – Tarragona – Sagunto

THE night train leaving the Gare d'Austerlitz for Toulouse and the Spanish frontier was of immense length and gave the illusion of being populated entirely by mutual friends. The dining car was a loud babel of voices. No mere Englishman could ever render the impression of their incessant talking. But even the ride to the station in a hired car had been full of excitement upon that spring evening early, for as the luggage was loaded we noticed police and *gardes mobiles* upon duty outside the Swedish Legation in the Avenue Marceau, we saw lights within shining from a room hung with tapestries upon the first floor, and knew that old King Gustaf had come here from his train to rest for an hour or two before continuing on his journey to the south of France. The king was a Bernadotte and the last surviving godson of the Emperor Napoleon III, who had welcomed him in person upon the first of his visits to Paris; and here he was, eighty years later, setting out once more for the Riviera. Had he been received by Napoleon under the gas lamps of the old Gare du Nord? – And we conjured up for ourselves the vision of the small Emperor in his frock coat and stovepipe hat, with his pale face and green eyes (he was already ill at that time), his waxed moustaches and little "imperial", standing in the midst of his military staff, with officers of the Guides and Hussards de la Garde around him, and the guard of honour formed by the huge Cent-Gardes in their white breeches, pale blue tunics and breastplates, and plumed helmets. Thence, into the Imperial carriages, into a *daumont* drawn by a pair of horses ridden by postilions in green liveries, and along the new boulevards to the Tuileries. How long ago it must have seemed to the old king!

This was a reflection that lightened the slow progress down fourteen coaches to the dining car, where we sat at a table with commercial travellers from Toulouse, and opposite the abbé and his sister with the classical profile and golden bracelets and earrings to match. Everybody knew everyone else, and there was much toasting in *petits verres* and passing on of jokes. Are there trains, we wondered, that start off as crowded as this, nightly, for the other provincial capitals? And we imagined ourselves in other moving towns of Frenchmen bound for Strasbourg, Brest, or La Rochelle. After dinner, on the way down the train, small children were slung from rack to rack in hammocks, and everyone was settling down to sleep. Toulouse was reached in the middle of the night, or, rather, early in the morning, but by the time it was daylight and we were nearing Perpignan – Perpignan that is so nearly Spanish and so near to Spain – the train was nearly empty and there was no one left on board to enjoy the morning sunlight. The Gascons of the night before who had been so voluble – I suppose they were Gascons – had vanished, and we were nearly alone when we reached the frontier at Port-Bou and found ourselves once more in Spain.

In Spain – but it is Catalonia and quite different, therefore, from the rest of Spain. The very soil is of another colour, some painter's palette of reds, it could be, for this is the red soil of the Balearics, repeated here upon the mainland, with the same rocks and fir trees. But there are rich vineyards, too, and green woods along the banks of streams. The first town of any importance is Figueras, where the Gitanos have their own suburb of shacks upon the outskirts, and there is little or nothing else of interest, except the Feria, with bull fights, which lasts for three days in May.[1] By now the Spanish train has already become fixed in its national habit of stopping at every station. An hour or two later we are nearing Gerona and it is time to stand in the corridor, for from the windows there is a magnificent view, in perspective, of the churches of Gerona: the cathedral with its Baroque frontispiece and flights of steps, and below it the octagonal Gothic

[1] And excepting the fact that Salvador Dalí is a native of Figueras.

tower of San Feliú with the broken pyramid of its spire, opposing and setting forth one another much in the manner of the thin steeple of St. Martin's, Ludgate, seen against the great dome of St. Paul's. This was Wren's forethought; and here, in Gerona, the architect in that theatrical age cannot have been unaware of the effect his façade and stairs would have with the work of the medieval builders for a foil, below. The Catalan Guillermo Boffiy was the genius of Gerona. It was he who built the great nave of the cathedral, which has the widest vault of any nave in Europe, but the wonders of Catalan Gothic are surpassed in aesthetic importance by the eleventh-century needlework tapestry of the Creation of the World, which has the added interest that it may be Saxon work from England.

Gerona apart, there is no more to delay us on our journey. The railway runs some miles inland from the Costa Brava, a stretch of coast which, with its bays and inlets and its sunny climate, may be the most beautiful part of the whole Mediterranean littoral, Capri and Amalfi excepted, and is as certainly to be preferred to the boring, jejune Antibes or to Juan-les-Pins. So indented is the coastline, so crowded with picturesque and varied incident, with secret sands and hidden grottos, that a clear view of much of its length is only to be had by cruising slowly along it in a boat. There is the promontory of Cape Creus with the little fishing port of Cadaqués at its extremity, and further on, passing by the Greek Rhoda, the town of Castellón de Ampurias with a church of the fourteenth century, and not far away the ruins of the Greek harbour town of Emporia, a Phocean settlement situated in ancient times upon an island, but now joined to the mainland. The Greek antecedents of this stretch of the Iberian coast are not, perhaps, sufficiently appreciated; and we may amuse ourselves, if we have the fancy, by remembering that this region was traversed by Hannibal upon his march on Rome, when he crossed the gap of the Col de Perthus within sight of the snow-clad Pyrenees, a thought which condones and even explains the painted elephants of José-María Sert in the cathedral at Vich (two sets of frescoes and two tribes of elephants, one destroyed during the Spanish Civil War and another completed

143

by the painter before his death!). And so, by way of San Feliú de Guixols, and an ever-increasing number of modern villas and hotels, to the huge and glittering Barcelona.

This is a town that, of a certainty, does not offer its charms at first sight of the stranger. It is, after Buenos Aires, the city with the largest Spanish speaking population in the world (and this if we agree that Catalan is their first or second language), and the first intimation of its beauties may come from the flower stalls along the Rambla. Here is the old quarter of the town and the cathedral, with gloomily beautiful interior; choir stalls of knights of the Golden Fleece; and Moor's head hanging below the organ. All this, and much else besides, must be taken for granted because of the darkness, but the cloister is a court of orange trees and sparkling waters. It has tall and old magnolia trees, a well house with carved stone bosses or roundels in its roof that are the perfection of late Gothic carving, and a pond or "canonical" with sacred geese like those of the Roman Capitol. Close by are the Audiencia and Diputación Provincial with medieval courts in Catalan Gothic, reminiscent of the Bargello and Palazzo Vecchio at Florence, but restored with a happier eye and lighter hand. Santa María del Mar, another of the wide-naved Catalan churches, is an empty shell and a mute witness to the Reds. Probably the most astonishing collection of primitive paintings in the world is to be admired in the great Exhibition palace in the gardens of Montjuich. They are installed in some twenty to thirty rooms, interspersed with early sculptures in painted wood and stone, and are to this extent more rare than the Sienese primitives in that they are Romanesque, not Gothic, and consist of fragments of the frescoed walls and apses from village churches in the Pyrenean valleys, transferred to plaster, work requiring an incredible degree of skill and patience. But a museum is a museum, anywhere and everywhere; as a collection the paintings have something of the deadening effect, and apart from the danger that the whole of an epoch of art could be destroyed by a single fire or by one act of war, it may be questioned whether it would not have been better to leave the paintings *in situ* in their inaccessible localities and to have made this a museum of copies. The Catalan primitives are, well and truly, a discovery of modern times. They were found, too, just at the time when modern painting and sculpture were turning, unknowingly, in those very directions. But the later development of Catalan painting is disappointing, except for Jaime Huguet, and by the time of Luis Dalmau, a Valencian painter who came under the influence of the Van Eycks, it has to be admitted that the Catalans have no early painter to equal the Portuguese Nuno Gonçalves, whose two triptychs at Lisbon are among the wonders of the Middle Ages. Barcelona, in our time, has been the town of Picasso and Salvador Dalí. It is easy enough to associate the first of these painters with Barcelona, for the poorer quarters or *banlieus* inspired him with the harlequins and acrobats of his "blue" period; but the "pale yellow sands" of Dalí,[1] his distant blue promontories and headlands, and the empty "old master" plains in his drawings, could be said to be derived, too, at a day's excursion from Barcelona.[2]

The church of la Sagrada Familia is not less peculiar than the most extreme works of Dalí or Picasso, more particularly when it is realized that it was begun as long ago as 1881, the year in which the latter painter was born. The architect Gaudí must be allowed talent or genius of an original order which could only be Spanish, and at that, Catalan, out of the whole of Spain. He guessed or anticipated the Art Nouveau, and then, at a longer hazard, Surrealism. Barcelona contains other extraordinary buildings by Gaudí. In one of the main streets is an apartment house built in the shape of the mountain of Monserrat, with waving balconies to suggest its dolomitic formations. A private house, opposite, simulates a breaking

[1] "On the pale yellow sands
There's a pair of clasped hands,
And an eyeball entangled in string,
And a bicycle seat,
And a plate of raw meat
And a thing that is *almost* a Thing."

Lord Berners.

[2] His golden sands are those of the seaside resort of Rosas, the Greek Rhoda.

wave: the walls surge wildly upwards, while the roof with its cresting of green tiles represents the foam and spray. I suspect that Gaudí, like Debussy, admired Hokusai's woodcut of the Great Wave! After this, his bishop's palace at Astorga, among the Maragatos, is "tame as tame". The Parque Güell, outside the town, is fantastic; at once a fun-fair, a petrified forest, and the great temple of Amun at Karnak, itself drunk, and reeling in an eccentric earthquake.

It is interesting in this modern town to be told that the café Suizo on the Rambla, now closed, was the same as one frequented by Casanova on his visits to Barcelona. And across the Rambla, under the same rood, are the club and opera house of the Liceo, with substantive and lavish furnishings of their period, huge oil paintings, stained windows, "dog-sinew" brackets and ornaments, Moroccan settees and inlaid tables, all the abracadabra of the 'nineties and the Art Nouveau, but a theatre that must be one of the most splendid of its kind in Europe, the many rows of gilded boxes, all upostered in crimson velvet, being as elaborate as the insides of coaches or old railway carriages, with seats at different levels as though to encourage talking during the music, high seats at the back like those in a dog cart, and a sort of mute inference of ices during the intervals and a champagne supper afterwards.

But Barcelona has other anachronisms to offer to our uncomplimentary age. It is a town where Cupid twangs his bow with blunted arrows; where swansdown is cottonwool; and the award of beauty, not a golden apple, but boxes of chocolates and marrons glacés. This is the procedure. After a dinner party in fashionable society a young man has to set forth, the next morning, and must find, in the first place, some suitable box, glass vase, or basket, or all three, after which he goes to the florist for flowers to put in the bowl or basket and to the chocolate shop for chocolates or marrons glacés, then, finally, to another shop where they will arrange the flowers, wrap up the chocolates and mount and decorate the whole affair with silken ribbons. We were told of a certain hostess who has been found with fifteen or twenty of these *pièces montées* upon the floor of her apartment after a dinner party. Nowhere else in Europe has the custom of floral tributes been carried to such exaggerated lengths. For our own part, in modesty, we left Barcelona with a bunch of Parma violets the size of a small cartwheel, two subsidiary bouquets or buttonholes dependant from its edges, and detachable, mere satellites of the main body of violets but reminiscent of the lesser flowerets of the old "hen-and-chicken" daisies, and a large box of marrons glacés. But the angle at which the Parma violets were posed upon the marrons glacés was something inimitable. It was elegant and raffish as the figures in a Beardsley drawing, and of the same period. The violets scented the inside of the motor, and for days to come perfumed the bedrooms in *albergues* and hotels. Other things besides gifts of flowers are lavish in Barcelona, including the size of the "helpings" in restaurants, which are twice as large, and fully twice as expensive, as in the best restaurants of London or of Paris. There are three or four restaurants, Parellada for instance, and another opposite it in the *Diagonal*, which must be as good as any in the world today, including one, down by the harbour, cleaner and whiter than any hospital, unexcelled for *paellas* and other traditional Spanish dishes, where you can see all the saucepans stewing in the kitchen and where the *patronne*, a lady of ample proportions clad like a vestal in pure white, but with the air and allure of a Phoenician goddess, with rouged fingernails and mascara'd eyes, will show you what is cooking, and lifting a particular saucepan lid tell you that the meat inside is from the bull killed in yesterday's bull fight.

The mountain of Montserrat, like Meteora, is among the marvels of nature, but the monastery is not be numbered among the most beautiful of the works of man. It is, in fact, hideously restored or renovated; and the mountain, not the monastery, is worth the short motor drive from Barcelona. How curious for an Englishman to find Augustus Hare, his countryman, warning him that "without having seen a fog no one should leave Montserrat"; and Hare goes on to speak of the shrubs that clothe the hillside, all evergreens, "which according to the old Spanish tradition, are permitted to bear their leaves all the year round, because they sheltered the weariness of the Virgin Mary and the Holy Child during their flight into Egypt". He tells of "cascades of honeysuckle, smilax, and jessamine", and of the troops of Suchet robbing and murdering "when they hunted the hermits like chamois along the cliffs". More Englishmen, with George Edmund Street, architect of our Law Courts, leading their front line, have poured out ecstatic praise of other Catalan churches. The Colegiata or Seo of Manresa is among the most splendid of these buildings, of golden yellow stone standing on a high rock, above a river, at the summit of its little town. Typical of a Colegiata, with no transepts, it gives the impression of the magnificent sketch of fragment of a master mind. But the interior, with fine rose window, one of the most gory of the Catalan Turk's or Moor's heads hanging under the organ, and a Florentine altar frontal of the fourteenth century in the sacristy, worked by Geri di Lapo, lacks, alas! the peasant women worshipping in large white flannel hoods upon their heads. To that extent was Street more fortunate in his day.

Lérida was another of Street's favourites. Situated on the main road between Madrid and Barcelona, it is a town through which most travellers hurry without another thought for the magnificent early cathedral high above their heads. This church was a barracks from the reign of Philip V, early in the eighteenth century, until 1948, and not long ago the nave was used for machine-gun practice and the aisles were dormitories. Now the church is undergoing fairly skilful restoration and the splendid carved capitals are being cleaned. Dating from the thirteenth century, the old cathedral is certainly one of the wonders of Spain. I find it more beautiful, for instance, than the monastery of Poblet, which is much more famous, because Poblet is a Cistercian Foundation following the beautiful but familiar pattern of Cistercian buildings in other countries in Europe, whereas Lérida has features which make it unique. It is a late Romanesque building with Gothic and Moorish influences. The carving of the capitals of the columns is of the first order or excellence; but, even in these, an Oriental hand is suspected, giving to them a freshness of handling which puts them in a class of sculpture to themselves. There are splendid carved portals, though not quite of the order of the capitals, and an immense cloister reduced by the military to heaps of rubble, but out of which, even now at this late date, some order is emerging. The whole building, ghosts of two centuries of conscript soldiers apart, has a vigorous militant, or masculine air about its planning and its sculpture, and is as important in architecture as any cathedral in Spain. At least, it has not been spoilt by restoration and it stands on its escarpment in one of the proudest situations of all Christian buildings.

Both Manresa and Lérida are inferior in scale to the huge nave or shell of Gerona, which in its daring construction is work more of an engineer than of an architect. The humourless, muddled mind of the mid-Victorian is apparent when Street continues, "In our large towns in England there is nothing we now want more than something which shall emulate the magnificent scale of these Catalan churches. They were built in the Middle Ages for a large manufacturing or seafaring population; and we have everywhere just such masses of souls to be dealt with as they were provided for."[1]

The most beautiful of Catalan buildings, there can be no question, is the cathedral of Palma de Mallorca, and in its wonderful setting by the blue waters of the Mediterranean many opinions may prefer it to any other Spanish building except the cathedral of Seville. How many more writers have compared it to some golden trireme or galleon about to raise anchor and move off into the bay! It is a conqueror's church, built by Jaime II of Aragon, who beat the Moors with his fleet of one hundred and fifty galleys, and in the excitement of his vic-

[1] It is, of course, the *tempo* of life that has altered and accelerated so much between Street's time and our own. An instance of which is afforded by one of the footnotes of his, in every other respect, most intelligent editor, where, describing the Episcopal Museum at Vich (full of wonderful treasures), it is advised that "the traveller will do well to provide himself with woollen socks and a footstove and to lay his plans to stay five days at least". Cf. *Gothic Architecture in Spain*, by G. E. Street, edited by Georgiana Goddard King, J. M. Dent & Sons, 1914, Vol. II, p. 149.

tory the nave is nearly twice as wide as any cathedral in our island and higher than any French cathedral except Beauvais. But those persons, most of them English, who would regard Majorca as a country apart, and Minorca, and still more Ibiza, as remote and lost islands because there is no time to visit them owing to the attractions of the mainland, must have it their own way. There is no space, here, for the red dolomites of Cap Formentor rising out of a purple sea; for Sóller and its little enclosed port or "concha"; or for Valldemosa and its memories of Chopin and Georges Sand; and we can but mention the circular court of the castle of Bellver; the happy valleys of the interior of the island, with their giant citrus and lemons and their carob trees; the old gardens of the manor houses; or even the old palaces and their courts or *patios* in Palma itself. For the Balearic Islands are a little world to themselves and our concern is with the mainland.

So we leave Barcelona by way of Sitges, a little resort "favourably known for its wine", with villas and tennis courts and roses, and a statue of El Greco, of all people, upon the promenade, and are bound for Tarragona. But, first, we make a detour in order to visit the famous monasteries of Poblet and Santas Creus. Nothing could exceed the luxuriant but forlorn beauty of the latter, for the cold stone is, quite simply, overgrown with flowers. A Cistercian foundation, modest, not exceptional in scale, with a picturesque village within its walls, cloisters in flower, and in the month of March violet-scented and loud with bees. In the church there are splendid alabaster, canopied tombs of the early kings of Aragon. It is hard to believe that it was only in 1835 that Santas Creus, and Poblet too, were sacked and burnt by mob violence during the Expulsion of the Orders. For Santas Creus lies sleeping, still . . . and Poblet? But the monastery of Poblet is that much more magnificent. It is among the most tremendous monuments of monkish hands. Alcobaça and Batalha are its only rivals – and, this is the moral, they should, also, be its warning. Those persons who, like the writer, remember all three of these monastries before they were restored must be fearful lest the fate of the first two overtake the last. For Alcobaça

150

and Batalha have been scrubbed and tidied till they are bare
as hospital wards and until the bare stone has lost the patina
of time. In the case of those monasteries in Portugal it has
been a vandalism nearly as effectual as the fire out of the clouds
that destroyed the Marienkirche at Lübeck. Batalha and Alcobaça have lost their beauty, and not content with that,
the restorers have taken away and removed everything of a
later date. Now Poblet has recently been given back to the
Cistercian monks, a decision which is entirely right, historically, and from the point of view of sentiment and of aesthetics.
The Cistercian monks in their white robes and pointed hoods,
so subtly differenced from the white Carthusians – and so
much resembling the Moors of Fez, for theirs too is a costume
that has come down, unaltered, from the twelfth century –
are in entire harmony with the pointed arches of the abbey
church. To its full beauty they are appropriate, indispensable,
indeed. But the side altars are now in process of rededication.
The stone walls of the church are being cleaned. It would be
better, surely, to leave them as they are. No further steps are
necessary than to repair the roof and keep out the rain. The
royal tombs, reconstructed from fragments, are already spoiled.
The beautiful little palace of Don Martín, and its outer stair,
are losing their fourteenth-century grace and elegance – are
losing their beauty while one looks at them, for it is evident
that they have been scraped and tidied. The cloister is beautiful
as ever. All lovers of Spain, while rejoicing that the monks
are back at Poblet, must hope that the wonders contained
within its mile-long battlemented wall will be treated with the
deliberation and gentle mercy that they deserve. For Poblet
is one of the buildings most instinct with poetry in the whole
kingdom.

And, coming down to the coast again, we are soon in the
golden light of Tarragona, a sort of golden or yellow luminos-
ity which clings to so many classical sites, which clothes the
cliffs of Posillipo, at foot of Virgil's tomb, and is golden as
honey at Syracuse. We would expect, immediately, from this
golden light that Tarragona was a Greek and then a Roman
city, and Tarragona was, in fact, the chief Roman town in

151

Spain. According to some authorities it had a population of a million in Roman times. We read that the Emperor Augustus resided here during the winter of 26 B.C., a precision of information that contrasts with the darkness of fifteen succeeding centuries of history. Augustus, no doubt, was enjoying just this golden light. He adorned the city with many buildings, theatres, circuses, and Roman baths, and the citizens, in return, put up a temple to Divus Augustus in his own lifetime – Augustus, it will be conceded, being a more worthy object of worship than the three workman tyrants of our time. Pliny, it is pleasant to read, praises the wines of Tarraco, the "vitifera Latelania", rivals of the Falernian; while Martial, when he speaks of the "aprica littora", means nothing other, surely, than this golden light we mention.

In course of time the Roman Tarraco became a heap of golden ruins and a quarry for the medieval builders. The cathedral of Tarragona is built, principally, from locks of Roman stone. It rises, in Catalan fashion, down the narrowest of streets, at the head of a splendid flight of steps, so that the beautiful rose window, and then the statues and doorways, reveal themselves, golden stone by stone. The interior is simple and magnificent, with its clustered columns, and the cloister one of the loveliest of all in this land of cloisters, the carved capitals forming an entire bestiary to themselves and a repository of the legend and humour of the Middle Ages. It is a beautiful experience to walk from the warm flower garden in this cloister, through rooms fuller than any curiosity shop, and to find oneself in front of a Gothic tapestry of the first quality, not inferior to those of Zamora or Zaragoza. Its theme is the Seven Virtues, or some subject akin to that: there are the sages of the ancient world enthroned under canopies; Eastern Kings, or the Three Magi; noblemen in Byzantine dresses with tall fur hats, like those of boyars; young ladies, of Gothic feature, in high steeple hats and wimples; and in the deep distance, high up, that is to say, a shepherd and his bagpipes. The foreground is thick with spring flowers, as was the cloister garden.

The particular climate of Tarragona continues for a stretch of some miles to either side of the city. The Roman ramparts of Tarraco are something memorable, while the still earlier Pelasgic or cyclopean walls and doorways are formed from blocks of stone as enormous as any prehistoric walls in Etruria – or in Peru. Nothing could be more evocative of the classical past than the Medol, a stone obelisk left standing by the Romans in a quarry, now become a grove of pines and cypresses, where Paul Casals has often played. It is a little distance out from Tarragona along the Roman shore of the blue ocean, among low vineyards and the red boughs of the pine trees. But the Roman illusion soon vanishes. We are coming to woods of orange trees, and soon after crossing the Ebro we are in another country, the kingdom of Valencia. Upon the left bank of the Ebro lies the old town of Tortosa, which, unfortunately, we had not time to visit. It has a cathedral with *sillería* (choir stalls) by Cristóbal de Salamanca; "the demon of Churriguerismo has been at work", and "the modern overdone organs", which Ford says "are sadly out of character", the treasury with a mention of ivory coffers, Arras tapestries, Limoges enamels, the episcopal palace, and the old houses and more churches, all point an invitation to Tortosa. At least, it lies in the low plain of the Ebro and must lack the drama and character of old towns in the high mountains.

But our route is down the coast to Valencia and beyond, and as far as Murcia. And not yet are there intimations of the warm-blooded South. Orange and pomegranate are few in number and far apart. Yet it is for an hour of the scented night that we drive, with frogs croaking in the ditches, before arriving at Benicarló, where there is another of the Albergues. The *langostinos* from this sandy shore are finer and bigger than any in Spain, or so it is easy to believe, dining off them fresh out of the lobster pots, and varying that diet during the next days with soles or other fish taken straight out of the sea. A mile or two away lies the fabulous Peñíscola, for it rises out of a bluer ocean like a more fabled Mont St. Michel, and with its legends of the Antipope Don Pedro de Luna could not be more aggressively and theatrically picturesque. But, in truth, there is nothing of any interest in Peñíscola. The vision is better than the reality, and it would be better not to climb up

153

the steep stone steps. Our other object in coming to Benicarló was in order to go to Morella, and this proved impossible because a bridge had been swept away and the road was broken.

Morella lies some fifty miles inland from the Mediterranean. It has Moorish walls and towers, and stands on a mountain peak below a Moorish castle, in midst of a circle of wild mountains. The topmost houses of this extraordinary town are often shrouded in clouds. Morella is out of the world altogether, and the *alforjas* (saddlebags) with woollen embroideries in bright colours, which are woven there, must help the illusion, for though of Moorish origin they recall the woollen *sarapes* of the Zapotec and Mixtec Indians in Mexico. There must be a strong Mudéjar element in the population of Morella, and the belt of Moorish walls and towers, the flat roofs, and the old castle touching into the clouds make of it a world apart.

But the green orange groves thicken, there are orchards of pomegranates, and the Roman light of Tarragona has become something different by the time we reach Sagunto, the ruins of which have the bloodstained distinction that they were the *casus belli* of the Second Punic War. Murviedro, the old name of the town, bears witness to its stony ruins, and the great Hannibal was wounded beneath its walls. It is now a dust-coloured town of indescribable picturesqueness, heavy with Roman ruins, climbing up, and ending in caves, under the walled hilltop, dust not of gunpowder but of the battering-ram and *phalarica*, of crumbled, not of exploded walls. But, as well, there are the beginnings of the whitewashed architecture of the South, Baroque archways that lead the way to little chapel under the shade of pine and cypress.

The ghosts of Sagunto, if such there be, must be spectral warriors, and we should expect to hear of the "hero's armèd shade" glittering in the cave mouths of the Gypsies, high up under the walls, whence there is that view down to the ruins of the Roman city. For long miles after we have left it behind Sagunto can be seen, but there is a dust cloud and a haze of heat hanging ahead over a distant city. Coloured domes and towers appear; we find a great concourse of people all hurrying in one direction, and are in the suburbs of Valencia.

154

2. VALENCIA, MURCIA

Fallas of Valencia – Murcia – Small Towns of the Levante

It is a sensation of an exciting order to enter a huge Southern town in the heat and blaze of noon and discover the entire population making for the centre of the city. But the day on which we arrived at Valencia was the third and last day of the Fallas, a local festival only inferior to the Feria of Seville, an occasion not to be compared to that in beauty, but a feast, above all, of noise and fireworks. There was the roar, even now, of squibs and firecrackers exploding at street corners, and soon, making our way slowly – for our motorcar had to fall in behind a band of music – we found the centre of a little square filled by an immense group of pasteboard sculpture.

It was a Falla; but the trouble with the Fallas is that they are all so ugly. They resemble the figures of a Neapolitan *presepio*, magnified, till they are larger than life-size, mounted upon platforms, and towering up in certain instances as high as the second-floor windows of the houses. They are caricature sculptures, made by the different parishes of Valencia in secrecy and mutual rivalry and set up, thus, in open competition; figures of workmen or housewives, municipal jokes, even, swollen of feature like the ventriloquist's dummy, and with the realistic detail of kitchen and workroom to add their waxwork horror to the dreadful puppets. The Fallas, in fact, darken the streets of Valencia with their ugliness and leave an unpleasant taste in the memory, but tonight is the climax or culmination when all over the town they will be set on fire and burnt to ashes.

The festival does not appear to be old in origin, but to have sprung up, unnoticed, as the diversion of the poorer streets and at last to have taken possession for three days of the whole town. The entire population is afoot, walking from one Falla to another, and comparing them. Among the crowd there are a number of young women wearing the local Valencian costume, silken dresses of green or brown, and golden headdresses with gilt pins, somehow recalling the golden mists of Valencia when the sun shines through the yellow dust, a costume not nearly so beautiful as that of the Sevillanas and lacking the grace of the high tortoiseshell comb and mantilla. Innumerable little girls are dressed more elaborately, but after the pattern of their mothers. But the male costume is no more to be seen, those voluminous white linen drawers (*zaragüelles*) which Ford compares to the *fustanella* of the Albanians, adding that "these are the small clothes which Augustus, when at Tarragona, put on in order to please the natives, as George IV did the kilt at Edinburgh". With the linen drawers was worn a velvet jacket, a silken sash, and their "long, lanky Red-Indian like hair was bound with a silken handkerchief, which looked in the distance like a turban". Their whole dress he describes as "antique and Asiatic", but to the writer it seems more akin to that of Naples.

Valencia is, decidedly, a city with an excitement and a beauty of its own. But the crowds were so thick, that afternoon, that it was out of the question to go sightseeing, and in fact we went to the bull fight and spent the late afternoon and evening in wandering along the streets. There were new Fallas at every corner, and one that was positively gigantic occupied nearly the whole of the Mercado, the huge square in the centre of the town. In the evening the sides of this square were lined with small children leaning up, half-asleep, against the buildings, waiting for the explosion which was due at midnight; and probably the only way in which to preserve something of the sullen, smouldering excitement of that last night of the Fallas is to describe our experiences of Valencia upon this and on a previous occasion many years ago as all taking place upon that selfsame day. The streets are thick, then, with fairground sculptures and loud with bands. Squibs are exploding all the time; and now and again a group of youths will run down the narrow streets, causing a regular fusillade, when everyone has to seek refuge in the open shops.

It was in these conditions of fire and gunpowder that we saw Valencia. One of the worst of the cannonades was in the little square in front of the Palacio de Dos Aguas, and when the smoke cleared, in the late evening light, we were able to appreciate the pale rose-and-green effect of this monument of the Rococo in Art Nouveau taste. For the Dos Aguas is in prophecy of the Paris Exhibition of 1900, of the Pont Alexandre III, and of Gaudí and the "new" architecture of la Sagrada Familia at Barcelona; yet it has all the graces of the eighteenth century. The sculptured portal is by Ignacio Vergara, and it could be compared to a Paris Exhibition version of the Atlantes doorways of palaces in Prague. The theme of the portal is not as far-fetched and absurd as might be imagined, for the pair of figures are the Dos Aguas, the "two waters", and the tribunal of peasants by whom their use is regulated holds its meetings nearby. There is a drawing of the scene by Gustave Doré; but if inclined to seek more intently for the origins of this curious architecture the mere detail that the church, nearby, was formerly a mosque may suggest a clue. In the year I visited it a low wall in the manner of a stockade surrounded the Palacio de Dos Aguas, and it was no easier than in 1925 to obtain entry. But the graceful windows of the first and second floor, once again, recalled the windows of the Prefettura at Lecce (though that is nearly a century earlier in date); while the wrought-iron grilles of the ground floor and, again, the many faceted balusters to the upper windows suggested Art Nouveau. What I had forgotten were the cupids standing above delicate "drops" between the top floor windows; the *oeils-de-boeuf* under the elaborate cresting; the corner towers like celestial pigeon lofts; and, more than all, the shimmering rose-and-green, sunset-after-rain colouring of the delicate and fanciful Dos Aguas.

But there was a roar of squibs and crackers, and making a detour in order to avoid this point of danger we found ourselves before the Rococo front of the cathedral. A German architect, Conrad Rudolf, had a hand in this, though it bears no resemblance to any German or Austrian building that I know. It is a concave front, like a three-leaved screen, with sculptured panels, built in a beautiful deep-golden stone. "Heavy" and "unsuccessful" are some of the terms in which it is abused. Ford calls it "a confused, unsightly jumble of the Corinthian order, with bad statues of the local saints". In reality, this is one of the prettiest of the Valencian buildings; and standing inside its railed forecourt, safe for a moment from the demon of the trams, one quickly appreciates the musical balance and perfection of its parts, due to the sculptor A. Vergara, "a pupil of Bernina" (*sic*) and father, apparently, of Ignacio Vergara. It is the interior of Valencia cathedral that is uninteresting and boring; nor does the stumpy Miguelete, its bell tower, redeem the dulness. Of more lively character is San Esteban with its memories of St. Vincent Ferrer, a Churrigueresque interior which is the scene of a curious ceremony on the Sunday after Easter, when in honour of the saint's baptism a group of fifteen or twenty life-size, dressed figures or *bultos*, in costumes of the period, and representing the priest, the sacristan, the viceroy and his wife, etc., are erected beside the font.[1] Evey hundred years (the last occasion was 1955) the miracles of St. Vincent Ferrer are represented in the open streets of Valencia, where altars are erected to the saint and "these exhibitions", we read – and we can believe it – "are so extraordinary that they must be seen to be credited".

Most wretchedly, another church, Los Santos Juanes, was burnt and destroyed during the Spanish Civil War for this had, perhaps, the richest interior in all Spain, in "Genoese style", but the enormous vaulted ceiling fresco by Antonio Palomino was an original and extraordinary work of art, proving that the "Spanish Vasari" had powers of imagination and execution far in excess of his contemporaries Lebrun or Sir James Thornhill. Los Santos Juanes, when I saw it, all those years ago, was blackened with age, but, like no other building that I have ever known, it recaptured the town life of the early eighteenth century in an ultra-Catholic town. As a personal memory I would compare it to the nun's church of San Gregario Ar-

[1] Amateurs of the poltergeist may be reminded of the "automatic" figures in the house of the Presbyterian minister, Dr. Eliakim Phelps, at Stratford, Connecticut. Cf. *Poltergeists*, by Sacheverell Sitwell, Faber & Faber, 1940, pp. 45–54.

meno in the slums of Naples. But I suppose, in the case of Los Santos Juanes, that this was the only occasion on which the dull Palomino was inspired, even as, on some golden summer evening in England, while the dragonflies yet dart and glitter, a heavy tench will rise out of the darkening pool and break the surface with an outsize ripple.

And the night hastens. And dead with fatigue, our ears deafened, our eyes smarting, our faces and hands – we scarcely exaggerate – blackened with the smoke and gunpowder from so many explosions, we had gone upstairs to bed, when, on the stroke of midnight, a continuous roar, beside which the blitz on London was no louder, brought one to the balcony. It was the last salvo of the fireworks and the burning of the Fallas, and to this ultimate series of explosions the gay Valencians have contrived to impart a crescendo the nature of which can only be indicated, automobilistically, in terms of supercharging or of the "cut out". The roar deepened and went into a higher gear; doors shook, walls trembled, one had to hold on the railing of the balcony. I have never heard so loud a noise in my life. The huge Falla in the Mercado went up in one crackling flame. There were fires in all the streets, and a crowd so thick that you could have walked upon their heads. The roar lingered, and shook, and shook again. Hector Berlioz, the master of massed drums and the augmented *batterie de cuivres,* would have wept deliriously, but, with vivid memories of bombed England, we went to sleep happy in the thought that no one was killed or injured and that the Valencians were but enjoying their yearly Fallas de San José.

Our proposal to tour the streets of the city only upon that last night of noise and fireworks proved, in the event, to be but a broken promise. It was because of the exceeding beauty of Valencia in the early morning – "early", that is to say, by Spanish standards, but, after such a night, there were few persons abroad by ten or half-past in the morning. So few, that one could stand away from the pavement, in the middle of the tram lines, in order to admire the equestrian group in bronze of St. Martin dividing his cloak with the beggar. This late Gothic sculpture is inset above a Baroque doorway, and curious it is, indeed, to see a theme, so appropriated to his own ends by El Greco, set forth, here in Valencia, with St. Martin like a young prince or page in a plumed cap, and the beggar not remote from those in early Flemish tapestries or paintings. And this trio of works of art – so typical of Spain – by a Fleming and by a Baroque sculptor, is made complete with the portrait of an archbishop, in a room upstairs, from the hand of Goya – all in this one church of San Martín.

But it is half-past eleven or twelve o'clock, nearly midday, and we have left till last what is in our opinion one of the beauties of Valencia, the hexagonal tower of Santa Catalina, built in 1688. At its foot is a market held in the centre of an entire circle of buildings, and it is wonderful to walk out from under the awnings of some pottery stall or toy stall and look up at the old tower. This round market place must date, at a guess, from the early years of last century, and it was an inspiration or, more probably, a happy accident that built this ring or circle below the tower and enabled one to admire an arc of its cornice, and tiled roof above, at play with the fretted edges of the octagon. This octagonal belfry is built in a dark golden stone, much weathered, and it has a richness and an intricacy that are Southern and Spanish – that are even Mexican – and that carry one, in imagination, to the twin towers of Taxco. The Palacio de Dos Aguas, the façade of the cathedral, the lost church of Los Santos Juanes, the tower of Santa Catalina, such, to my taste, are things typical of Valencia, more so, if I dare say this, than many admirable paintings by Ribalta and Ribera, and local Primitives, in the museum. For Valencia is a city with living character, like Naples. There are good paintings of the Valencian festivals by Sorolla, and the Feria at the end of July may be more beautiful as a spectacle than the Fallas, for temporary booths and kiosques are put up along the Alameda, there are floral games and processions – *Jochs florals* in the local dialect – and splendid bull fights.

The domes and towers of the city appeared to wonderful advantage over the river, as we drove away, bound for the lagoons and marshes of the Albufera. This was the duchy given by Napoleon to Marshal Suchet, with its Arab name. "The see and throne of Flora and Pomona", Ford calls it, in one of his few phrases that are unjustified, for its interest lies, really, in its fish and waterfowl. Rice is cultivated all around the Albufera, giving some notion of the celestial paddy fields in the old Confucian China, as we see the peasants paddling, ankledeep, in the water and thick mud, or the immature green rice growing in a thin grass, as it used to grow, in childhood's days, upon the bald head of the phrenologist's clay bust. Characteristic of this strange region are the whitewashed *barracas* or fishermen's huts with steep, thatched roofs. This magic name, which reminds us of the booths and sideshows of the Feria at Seville, here denotes something that is typically Valencian. It recalls or revokes Valencia, and as a poetical or pictorial symbol we would give it the importance of the cubical, whitewashed box of Pulcinella under the tall vines of Aversa, in the plain of Naples. Many and many are the white *barracas* gleaming here and there, and into the distance, and there is a whole village of them on an island in the Albufera, at Palmar, to which the Valencians row out in order to enjoy a *paella valenciana*, made of rice and eels and shellfish from the shallow waters.

But the Albufera fades out of sight, like a mirage, and after a few more miles we reach Gandía. The Colegiata, here, has suffered much injury during the Civil War, and the only interest is the palace of the Borjas with its few state rooms of the late seventeenth century decorated in gold and colours by Gaspar de la Huerta in saintly, fairground style. There are many relics of the Jesuit San Francisco de Borja, fourth Duke of Gandía, who was converted from a worldly life by his horror at the sight of the corpse of Isabella of Portugal, wife of the Emperor Charles V, with whom it is surmised he had been in love. It was his official duty to accompany her funeral cortège from Toledo to Granada, where her coffin had to be opened in order to identify her body in presence of the civic authorities – a legend so dramatic that we would not pursue it further lest it should prove not to be true. Our road led, hence, along the coast; but Játiva, the other Borja town, lies some miles inland, and according to all accounts, has fountains and palaces, and churches in which use is made of the local pink and red marbles. Alcoy, another town some fifty miles to the south, has churches "in the local Valencian style", which means a picturesque surge of houses up a steep ravine, and the tiled dome of the Iglesia Mayor and its hexagonal tower, much in the style of Santa Catalina. But we kept near to the Mediterranean, and presently were descending some slight hills with loggia'd farmhouses, in which we could see the geraniums growing, towards a rock or hill of extraordinary shape, rising, apparently, straight out of the ocean. This was the Punta or Cape of Ifach, one of Spain's natural wonders, except that, at Ifach, it is difficult to believe one is in Spain. It is a rock, two or three hundred feet high, with a low shore connecting it to the mainland; a hotel, a few fishermen's cottages, and a Lilliputian harbour. Ifach, according to Rhys Carpenter, is the Greek Hemeroscopeion. And its landscape is so classical and simple that it reduces, in drawing, to a few mere lines. The rock, above, is inaccessible, the sickle shore curves round to it, and in the fires of sunset there is nothing else but the waist-high horizon and dark purple ocean. In fact, it is difficult to grasp the true dimensions of that landscape, so classical are the proportions. If you look out at it, at midnight, it lies in a line or two, but darker and more mysterious, and you may think the ghosts of that civilization inhabit the bare bones, so Hellenic are that beauty and that harmony. How remote from Ifach are the fandango and mantilla! A white wall or the shade of a column are enough inhabitants. In the light of morning that rock and that empty ocean are an invitation to embark – for Syracuse or past Cape Sunium? You expect the beak of a trireme round the high rock, or the sail of a Greek fisherman. But in a few moments you are among the groves of orange trees, in Spain once more, and on the road to Alicante.

This is a town with a straight street running down to the palm trees and the harbour, with sea and palm trees below the window of the restaurant, a graceful Churrigueresque doorway to a church in the blazing sunlight, shops selling *turrón de Jijona*, a most delicious sweet made of almonds, in little wooden packing cases complete with nails; more palms and blue sea, and again, more sea and palms. Alicante could hardly be pleasanter, or more delightful, or less interesting. But it is only half an hour, by road, from Elche, in a forest of palms as dense as that of Marrâkesh. To the African aspect of Elche must be added the memory of the "Dama de Elche", the only work of art of the Iberian epoch that is left to us. That peaked, sacerdotal headdress of a sacred prostitute, or virgin, those huge cartwheel earrings, would not be out of place in Elche, a town which has one of the most astonishingly elaborate and graceful façades in all the Levante, built in that local style that is neither quite Rococo nor Churrigueresque, but more poetical than the one and saner and more balanced than the other. It is in this church that the miracle play of Elche is performed, every year in August, a religious ceremony as curious as any in Christian Europe and a procedure as "set" and formalized as that of the dancing white Lippizaners in the Winter Riding School at Vienna, It is an *auto-da-fé* or sacred play in the old Limousin or *langue d'oc* dialect, of which Elche is the most southern or ultimate extension. There are picturesque processions through the town, and at the climax of the play Baroque cupids in the form of living children are lowered from the ceiling.[1] It is a rustic masque of which the setting should be the old Teatro Farnese at Parma, where, till lately, the stage machinery for clouds and winds was still in being. But at Elche there is nothing Italian; it is Moorish.

The next town to the south is Orihuela, where, it was during Holy Week, a most impressive service was being held in the church of Santo Domingo. There were numbers of canons in scarlet and purple silk, and bottles and tumblers with lumps of sugar in them and a white-coated waiter in attendance in the sacristy, all of which we noticed on our way to see the painting of the Temptation of St. Thomas Aquinas by Velázquez, probably the only picture by the master in any church, but a most disappointing experience, although accepted by the authorities as genuine. This church of Santo Domingo has two

[1] The music is attributed to Ginés Pérez de Orihuela, who was composer and organist to Valencia cathedral in 1581, but the melody may be of the thirteenth century.

splendid, double-storeyed cloisters; but the rest of the way, and indeed, all that and all the previous day, had led through orange groves so beautiful in scent and as a spectacle of abundance that they banished all other admirations and allowed for little more memory than the heaped fruit in the shadow, or the red globes upon the trees. The orange groves had been particularly beautiful, the previous evening, upon the road to Ifach, but now, nearing Murcia, they seemed to surpass themselves.[1] Gone alas! are "the dusky countrymen in their white *bragas* and striped *mantas*, looking like Greeks"; and leaving the kingdom of Valencia, now, for that of Murcia, no longer do we pass the old men in black stocking caps, velvet jackets, black kneebreeches, and white stockings, living relics of the eighteenth century, who walk slowly, leaning heavily upon their sticks. But there are lorries by the roadside; high stacks and pyramids or oranges under the trees; the aloe hedges are constellations of spiked clubs or of flat turtle fins armed with prickles, and multiplying, almost, while you look at them. The palm trees are African, and in their element of blue fire and sand. There are bamboo glades, what we presume to be sugar canes, and pomegranates. And the heavenly orange groves to either hand, with a distant view of coloured domes and towers.

This is Murcia, a town of the South which I have wanted to visit all the sensible years of my life, to the extent that I called one of my first poems *The Mayor of Murcia*. When we arrived in the late afternoon a crowd was walking up and down the Paseo de la Glorieta along the river. There were clipped trees, a bandstand, gaily dressed nurses and their charges, conscript soldiers, and not a few of "dark children of the Zend", all in the ochre sunlight, with golden buildings to one side, the foaming weir to the other, and a fair down at the far end of the Glorieta, under the trees, with swings and roundabouts and the blaring of the steam organ. All upon a rustic or bucolic scale. And the Glorieta is continued, in the other direction, along the terrace of the Malecón, a dyke or embankment which runs for half a mile or more at the level of the loaded

[1] As late as 1882 there was no means of conveyance for the four leagues between Orihuela and Murcia but a small springless cart.

orange boughs, with gardens below it, a Botanical Garden, and more palm trees. This Malecón, this terrace of cement and sand, had the youth and beauty of the town massed down its entire length, with, in prospect, the blue domes of Murcia.

At the back of the hotel there are a dozen or twenty hooded carriages, or *tartanas*, drawn up, waiting. Let us, admiring the polished brass and pretty woodwork, climb into one, sit sideways, and drive round the town! In summer, we are told, awnings or *toldos* are hung across the streets from house to house. But it is not hot enough, today, and not too hot to get down in order to look at the shop window in the Calle de Platería, the Murcian Sierpes, where no wheeled traffic is allowed. And it was in this manner, for it is now morning, night having faded into sleep to the music of the steam organs and the softer music of the weir, that we come out of the beginning of the Platería, in order to admire the façade of the cathedral: this is a masterpiece of "decadent" architecture.

In all Spain its only rival is the west front, El Obradoiro, of Santiago de Compostela. This beautiful flight of architecture could be described as an epitome or embodiment of the warm South, and it does really possess the rare quality of movement. Ford, who speaks of it as "rising in compartments, like a drawn-out telescope", was evidently conscious of this, but it more nearly resembles a peepshow or the proscenium of a toy theatre. Seen down one of the narrow, dark *calles* that lead towards it, standing out in full sunlight in the middle of its square, the red-gold façade looks too unsubstantial to be built of stone. Structurally, it appears to be lifted or held up from behind, and is, to this extent, "a theatrical composition", though little related, as another writer would have it, to the style of Borromini. It consists of wings, in diminished storeys, and a hooded frontispiece. The lower order is Corinthian, and there are projecting pairs of fluted columns, supporting more columns above, and carrying one half of the broken architrave, which is to say, one segment of the golden hood. The central door is set back with fluttering cornices and there is a profusion of sculpture and statues, everywhere, on the sky-line, under canopies, and in niches. Beautiful features are the

165

winged angels riding the curving volutes; and it may be said of all the sculpture that it grows out of, and is not imposed upon, the stone. The architect was the little known Jaime Bort, who designed the façade in 1737, and who deserves to be remembered with Fernando Casas y Novoa, architect of El Obradoiro, begun in the next year, as the most elaborate and graceful of architectural draughtsmen of the later age. Nowhere more so, at Murcia, than in the lovely sidewings of this theatre scene, which take the form of rounded cylinders, of rolled parchments in their boxes, for that is the effect of the red-gold stays or buttresses which peg down the scene, and which are given cupolas like little well heads or sentry boxes, and are enlivened and given flight by architect and sculptor. It is a façade intended for sunlight, that is beautiful at all hours of day, and, I doubt not, by moonlight, and that is in complement to the high and commanding tower. But the interior of the cathedral is uninteresting. Murcia, like many another southern town, is more beautiful in its streets and squares than from within.

This is of a particular application here, because of the *pasos* or groups of sculpture that are carried round the town in Holy Week, and that are even more dramatic in gesture and characterization than the *pasos* of Seville. There had been a procession at midnight, and we had seen the scarlet *penitentes*, torch in hand, crossing the river to the church of Carmen with one of the great *pasos* of Salzillo in their midst, and had heard the low, discordant trumpet. But, now, it was Good Friday and there were to be more processions. The sculptures of Salzillo were to be carried to every quarter of the town, and we reached the Ermita de Jesús, just in time, before the most famous of his statues were taken out into the street. It is a circular chapel with the sculptures of Salzillo exhibited on platforms in little rooms or cells leading off from it. There is a Last Supper with the disciples sitting at table on stools "with cabriole legs", and Christ seated in a Chippendale chair, a scene that resembles a petrified variant of El Greco's paintings of The Last Supper, but with the figures turned to wood, not stone, an Agony in the Garden, a Scourging, and a Bearing of the

Cross. The figures are dressed in stuffs and velvets. The sculptor Francisco Zarcillo, or Salzillo, was son of a Neapolitan, born at Capua, and during his lifetime (1707–1781), together with his sister and his brothers, is said to have carved a total population of four thousand wooden figures. These *pasos* in the Ermita de Jesús are his most famous works. There are critics who recognize his hand in some of the statues on the cathedral front, but wood was his chosen material. Salzillo was the carver of Neapolitan *presepio* figures in excelsis, and beside the many other works by him in Murcian churches, and his carvings in towns near by, there is a *nacimiento* or crêche by Salzillo, a perfect instance of the *presepio*, in the museum at Murcia, with three hundred and seventy-two animals and one hundred and eighty-four little figures of peasants by his hand.

Processions were forming even as we left the Ermita de Jesús. The streets full of *penitentes* and of "Pharisees" dressed in purple with flat caps. It was the day or hour of Salzillo; but a minor horror attaches to his carved figures because they are two-thirds life-size, "life-size" meaning average height, so that they are not much taller than dwarfs or pygmies. Wood is like wax to Salzillo's chisel; his figures are hysterically real; and when finished they were painted with something of the embalmer's or of Madame Tussaud's horrid art. It must be remembered, of course, that they are processional figures intended to be seen from far away. During the week there were to be processions at nearly every hour of the day and night; Murcia being as fervent in this respect as Seville, and, according to some opinions, more religious still. And the mourning wail of the nocturnal trumpet is louder than in Seville; the trumpets are even trailed through the streets in little chariots. But there are secular as well as sacred celebrations; upon Easter Sunday (*Domingo de gloria*) a *gran corrida de toros* in which will be fought from horseback, *será rejoneado*, a young bull, *un novillo* by the Excmo. Señor Duque de Pinohermoso, together with six bulls from a famous *ganadería* of Salamanca, by the matadors Pepe Luis Vázquez, Antonio Bienvenida, and Manuel Escudero (all famous names of matadors), "con

167

sus correspondientes cuadrillas", which means with their respective bands of four assistants. And in the local morning paper I read that on Easter Monday there will be a great bull fight in Cartagena, featuring a woman bull fighter and that a special train for the *aficionados* will leave for Cartagena in the morning, returning to Murcia in the evening after the bull fight. And there could be many a less pleasant way of spending the afternoon and evening, I thought, than with the *aficionados* of Murcia, a town I have loved to think of for thirty years, since I first wrote poetry. . . .

But our journey was not yet finished. We had to go on that afternoon to Lorca and beyond, past more aloe hedges, by more palms and pomegranates, where in a few weeks the gigantic sunflower would nod its parhelion head, where the peasants in the fields still wear white handkerchiefs on their heads and "are dusky as Moors", but the women no longer wear the Murcian costume of blue *sayas* and yellow bodices. And Lorca is one of the prettiest of little southern towns. It is a Murcian Noto, but without the balconies supported upon figures of Turks or Chinamen, or pierrots or winged pegasuses, that are the beauty of that country town in Sicily, among the orange groves. Lorca, nevertheless, has a palace of the Guevara's, of 1693, with twisted, Salomonic pillars and balconies with iron grilles, and the whole town is full of little churches and convents and old houses. The Colegiata has a superb Baroque façade, with as much "movement", but more bucolic, than the façade of Murcia. The smaller churches have carvings and *pasos* by Salzillo and another sculptor, Roque López. The town is divided into two factions, the "Whites" and "Blues", who rival with each other in their processions during Holy Week and often come to blows. And the processions are different in nature from those of Murcia. The population become actors; they are characters from the Old Testament, Roman soldiers, allegorical tableaux drawn along on platforms, and anomalies such as winged angels in robes and long blonde wigs riding on horseback. The long trumpets resound, like conches, from every quarter of the town.

But the inhabitants of Lorca, exhausted by enthusiasm, are

not equal to such exertions every year. There was the usual crowds of *penitentes*, but this year the population was not acting. It was a season of what Italian operatic companies call *riposo*. And walking round Lorca, looking in the churches, I came to connect in my imagination the special train that took the *aficionados* of Murcia to the bull fight at Cartagena with the arrival of Salzillo and his brothers and sister and their assistants ("sus correspondientes cuadrillas") in one of these little towns, Lorca, Orihuela, Mula, Yecla, Jumilla. How I would have liked to arrive early upon the platform of the railway station at Murcia; to choose my companions; sit with them in the crowd; and return with them in the evening, talking all the way! Salzillo and his painters and gilders, his hewers of wood, must be looked upon as the animators of Murcia, Lorca, and the other little towns. To a greater degree than Martínez Montañés, Alonso Cano, Pedro de Mena, or the other polychrome sculptors, Salzillo is the master of the *paso*. Their *forte* was the single figure, his, the group. But it is probable that we shall admire the processions without liking the sculptures, which is equivalent to the ordinary Englishman's attitude towards the bull fight. Lorca, with its steep streets and whitewashed houses, its escutcheons and innumerable convents and little chapels, is an inspiring and beautiful little town. But our way led twelve miles further on, along a road bordered with pine trees, to a familiar white building with semicircular diningroom and pillared colonnade and clean bedrooms above, another of the *Albergues*, that of Puerto Lumbreras, which we made our centre for a stay of several days.

Like all of the other *Albergues* it lies about a mile out from a little town, a place of no interest except for a few cave dwellings, but Puerto Lumbreras is upon the main road from Murcia to Almería and to Málaga. And having had to sacrifice Morella at an earlier stage of our journey, owing to a broken bridge, we were anxious not to miss Mojácar, a town of the same Mudéjar character, about fifty miles from Puerto Lumbreras, in the province of Almería, near the sea. The road led through the mining town of Cuevas de Vera (silver and lead mines), but I had confused this with another town of similar name where there are Gypsies living in caves, and was disappointed. Or rather, I was misinformed. The Gypsy settlement at Cuevas de Vera is second only in interest to that at Guadix. There is no other town of the same name. It is a little distance, thence, down to the sea, at a place which is an entire scene of desolation, with ruined factories down by the seashore, houses which have been burnt out and deserted, and but a goat or two to crop the weedgrown streets. The town ends in something that resembles a ghostly coastguard station; the road runs along the side of that and ends in nothing. But it reappears again, and leads off with an improved surface, at a sharp angle, inland. A conical hill comes into view on the left with some dark lines and shadows near its summit. We come to another village and ask for Mojácar and are on the wrong road. We have to go back again to the coastguard station, where there is no road at all, and straight down into a riverbed. Mojácar now appears high upon its conical hill with no means of getting to it. But there is some kind of rough track, strewn with heavy stones, that winds towards it through more riverbeds, and eventually into a fertile valley. Towns like La Alberca, like Morella, like Mojácar, can only exist by virtue of the fertile country round them.

We pass a farm, but it looks more like some painter's dwelling, quite literally, "smothered with bougainvillea" from floor to ceiling. A few peasants come by on donkeys, and Mojácar suddenly appears, immediately in front, but in so precipitous a situation that it is difficult to believe in it. And we come, at the foot of the hill, to a large open air washing place or laundry. From here the road begins climbing. It winds round the hill of Mojácar without wall or parapet, with a view that is soon dizzying from its immensity, and that owing to its scale is exactly like looking down from an aeroplane. It is curious, too, that the houses of Mojácar are not yet in sight. You have to climb right to the top of the hill before you see them, when you come out into some kind of a town square or *plaza*, and the houses are there below you, sloping down the other incline of the mountain. Not that there is anything interesting in Mojácar in the way of buildings, but its situation is so extraordinary. The houses are completely flat-topped; the alleys are so steep that they are more like stairways. The women of Mojácar, one and all, wore yellow blankets in the manner of shawls, covering their heads and shoulders, some a pale yellow and others a yellow that was darker or more saffron, but yellow was evidently the fashion in Mojácar, and one wondered when, and why, the fashion started. They had no other trace of local costume, but the yellow blankets were ubiquitous and on every female head. The men of Mojácar were dressed in an ordinary way, like Spanish peasants anywhere. Nevertheless, this community of two or three thousand persons, which is entirely isolated, miles from anywhere, without even a road leading to it, with no railway nearer than Almería, and not making any use at all of the sea, which is so near, must have an interior life of its own that grows in upon itself. And if a great proportion of the "Moorish" population of Spain were Spaniards turned Moslem, there are a few little towns, like Morella or Mojácar, where the opposite is true and the inhabitants are Moors from five centuries back, gone Christian. Such, too, we would infer are the people of La Alberca, though, it is probable, not Moors but Berbers.

There are, of course, other places with a strong Moorish influence along this coast of Spain that is in front of Northern Africa. The veiled women of Vejer de la Frontera, between Cádiz and Gibraltar, are an instance. The black "nuns" of that brilliant whitewashed town, whitest of all Southern towns, with its *patios* of roses and geraniums, in sight of Africa, we have compared to the women of Sallee, in Morocco, who walk stealthily, robed from head to foot in white, like Carthusian nuns or white nuns of the Cister, like a band or sisterhood of Cyclop women. We had been told of another village, Abarán, near Cieza, where the road climbs from Murcia, on the way back to Madrid, and took the opportunity of going there, on our return. Abarán is a place where the women were veiled entirely, like Moslem women, until the outbreak of the Spanish Civil War. It lies, under jagged peaks of rock, in an oasis of incredible fertility, with orange and lemon groves and many carob trees. And, here, a curious and terrible spectacle of

171

misery presented itself at the far end of the straggling town, where there was a dirty pond by the roadside and three boys, between eight and twelve years old, came running up to beg. One of them wore a woman's sheepskin jacket, hardly covering his thighs, and, except for this, he and the other boys were entirely naked. Their faces were pinched with hunger; their ribs were showing; they were, obviously, half-starving. Moreover, as I could see for myself, they were Spaniards, not Gitanos. A few yards away there was the body of a dead mule in the middle of the road. I had been told of other naked children in villages in Andalucía and of a whole group of them down at El Grao, the seaport of Valencia, but naked children are a horrible and a disgraceful sight, anywhere in Europe. At Abarán they appeared, too, to be half-witted; and the local authorities should be censured for allowing this sordid shame to be seen in public.

At Mojácar, happily, there was nothing of the kind. The children were, in fact, remarkably beautiful. A little girl, Antonia, eight years old and too young, therefore, to wear the yellow blanket, who followed us up and down the precipices of the town with her friends, was a pattern of Spanish beauty and good manners. Not much can be wrong with a town where the children are so good looking. There is a house at the top of Mojácar which has balconies with great pots of roses and geraniums and bougainvillea. You turn a corner and see it, and have to climb down lower and look up at it from an angle. It has several floors of flowering windows, and a terrace. I asked at the blacksmith's and was told it was the doctor's house and that his hanging garden was as beautiful as this at all seasons of the year. Is it this doctor who is responsible for so much visible absence of disease at Mojácar? He must have happy mornings and evenings among his flowers, looking down upon that roadless plain. How do letters get to Mojácar? How do medicines ever arrive there? But we contrived, somehow, to achieve the journey back without mishap, up and down the shoals and shingle banks of the riverbeds, returning late in the afternoon to Puerto Lumbreras in good time for the early start, next day, for Guadix.

172

25 Mallorca: the cathedral and harbour of Palma

26 Costa Brava: repairing nets at Rosas

27 Ansó, Aragon: a church procession

29 The Escorial: bronze group of Charles V and family, by Pompeo Leoni

28 Madrid: the Escorial, begun in 1563

30   Barcelona: the unfinished church of la Sagrada Familia, by Gaudí

31   Costa Brava: a fisherman of Puerto de la Selva

32   Madrid: a bull fight

3. BARRIO DE SANTIAGO

Gypsy Caves at Guadix

There was a lure beyond the golden façade of Murcia, the processional idols, and *alameda* loud with flowers. And the bright light beckoning was the Gypsy caves at Guadix. I know now, what I had always thought, that Guadix must be the most wildly picturesque settlement of the Gypsies in all Europe. Nowhere can there be human habitations stranger or more peculiar than the Gypsy suburb of the Barrio de Santiago. I had wanted to go there ever since I first went to Granada – for Guadix is more easily reached from Granada – but now, at last, here was the opportunity, and we had come through Murcia, on purpose, to Puerto Lumbreras, in order to make the journey the long way round.

It was raining – the only day it rained – and a soft wind was playing in the pine boughs, and the road turned down the valley below the cliff dwellings, and climbed into a wilderness of flat hills, out of Spain altogether, and more resembling what one had heard and read of Persia. We had, now, left the province of Murcia and were in the kingdom of Granada. We passed a flat hill, the whole top seam of which, under the surface, to the length perhaps of a quarter of a mile, had been hollowed and scooped out to form human dwellings. This was down a *barranco* or ravine with a few crops and fruit trees. Otherwise, the desolation was unbroken. During winter, in wind or rain, it must be the howling wilderness. But the bareness of such a landscape, provided one passes quickly enough through it, is stimulating to thought.

There were places where the road was cut out of the soft sandstone and pillars, like obelisks, had been left standing by the side. Far away in the distance there was a considerable town, probably Baza, with the "rose-planted *alameda,* and women who are among the prettiest in Spain. They are fair-complexioned, and clad in green *sayas* with black stripes and red edgings; their feet are sandalled, their step elastic, and they carry baskets and pitchers on their heads in a classical manner." That was a hundred years ago. But we turned our backs on Baza and climbed higher into the desert of soft stone and clay. And in this manner two and a half hours went by until, turning a corner, the snowy slopes of the Sierra Nevada came into sight, much as you see them from Granada, hanging in the sky above the other mountains and with their bases hidden. And now the road started upon a long winding descent, straightening out, eventually, into a direct run of some miles towards low hills that were mysteriously flat and level, like cloudbanks on an evening after rain, and towards a long, low line of jagged peaks, or edges. Now, and at last, the road pointed to a town, lying in utmost simplification, just a far-off town and a building that must be a church, immediately under, it seemed, the snows of the Sierra Nevada.

It was Guadix. But we had decided to pass it by, for the moment, and go straight on to Purullena. And, in the meantime, those extraordinary jagged peaks or hillocks began to shed their mystery. For driving up to the gates of Guadix we took the road leading to the right, towards Granada, and were soon passing the beet fields and coming into the heart of the Thebaid. It extends particularly to this side of the town of Guadix, and consists of clay hills worn down by wind and water into the strangest and most contorted spires and pinnacles. Having seen it, I cannot agree that it "resembles a stormy sea whose waves have been suddenly transformed into solid substances". For it much more peculiar than that; but you do not see it in all its wildness at the moment. You come to an end of it, and there are green fields of wheat and mulberry trees.

But Purullena is a lesser Guadix and Purullena is at hand. It is but three miles from Guadix. The road comes over the brow of a soft clay hill, and down into a circle or rather a pair of amphitheatres extending to both sides. These are the caves of Purullena, and at first glance they remind one of the long Primitive painting of Monks in the Thebaid, by Pietro Lorenzetti, that used to hang in the first room of the Uffizi. But this comparison, I am aware, is of no use to those who do not know this picture. The hills, or high banks, of Purullena

174

are in the painting, with little houses built into them and hermits at the mouths of their caves. But a Gypsy woman comes out of one of the caves and the Thebaid is forgotten. Children collect from nowhere, and the wind raises hurricanes of dust.

The caves have whitewashed fronts and rise at different levels in every direction to both sides of the road. But the caves of Purullena are scooped out of flat banks of earth; they are not hollowed out of hillocks that are, themselves, the shapes of tents or turrets. And this, as we shall see, is the difference between the Gypsy caves of Guadix and those of Purullena. In many parts of Spain, as the reader of this book will know by now, there are these cave dwellings. Perhaps Purullena is only more sensational than many others because the road goes through the middle of it. The caves are in a circle with a flat skyline, which is formed from the low hills, like cloudbanks, that we saw from afar. It is said that Gitano dress is to be seen at its purest in Purullena, when there is a wedding, but many of the inhabitants are peasants who work in the beet fields, not Gitanos. At night, if you drive through it, Purullena must look extraordinary with the lights shining from the doors of all the caves. But it can only be sensational to those who have not seen the Barrio de Santiago, and after a few moments we turned back to Guadix.

The cathedral has choir stalls in Churrigueresque style in red wood, that look brand new. They recall the *sacristía* of the Cartuja at Granada with fluttering cornices and fretted pilasters, and are one of the few things in Spain that suggest a direct influence from Mexico.[1] And that is all. There is nothing else in Guadix. But trouble begins when you ask for the Barrio de Santiago. For it is not known by that name. It would be possible to be in Guadix and miss it altogether. No one has heard of it, and they all shake their heads. And if you ask for the Gitanos they point vaguely and look doubtful. Upon the strength of this many persons would give it up and go away. It was in this manner, getting but negative answers to our questions, that we had missed the Gypsy caves at Cuevas de la Vera. And having been bold the direction of the Barrio,

[1] By Torcuato Ruiz del Peral.

we went, expecting little or nothing for our pains. It would be, in all probability, a few cave dwellings under a hill, like those of the Morería and the Camino de la Soledad at Calatayud. Less exciting, in all likelihood, than the caves of Purullena.

The Barrio de Santiago is at the back of Guadix, right behind the town. It gives the impression of being directly under the Sierra Nevada. There is no sign of it at all in Guadix. You go up to the back of the town where the road stops, and even then may be heading in the wrong direction, for some sort of track continues into the country, and would take you right past the entrance to the Barrio. The houses begin to be white-washed and one-floored, that is all, and a narrow rocky lane leads in and out among them, and begins to climb. Soon there are houses no longer, but whitewashed cave fronts with little courts in front of them, the size of the areas of old London houses, and with pots of roses and geraniums. One or two have vines on trellises now coming into leaf. There are rocky paths leading up behind these "luxury" cave dwellings, but no sign, yet, of the Gitanos.

You come to the top of a little hill, where the road dips, and suddenly see before you the caves of the Barrio de Santiago. It opens right out before you, as though you were looking down into a circus, and you have only to come down a few steps lower and you are in the middle of the biggest Gypsy cave town, and probably the largest troglodyte population, in the world. I have no idea how many persons are living in the caves of the Barrio de Santiago, but it would be no sur-prise to be told that it has five or six thousand inhabitants. And the town is continually opening out into new directions. One has to decide at an early stage to keep to the path that leads straight ahead, for it branches off and one path goes to the left into another part of the Barrio, and works round and back again into what we would like to call the main amphi-theatre of cave dwellings, which we have not yet even seen. A girl with an indescribably dirty face – I think the dirtiest face that I have ever known, with the dirt and grime of all her years since childhood superimposed upon her tawny skin – comes running down a rocky pathway. She has the snake-like locks of the true Gypsy and an insolent, terrible manner as though hustling prisoners to their execution, and I would have written "criminals", but that the instincts of such a creature would be surely upon the side of crime. Accompanying her are two young men, with faces like Red Indians, clothed in rags of shirts and trousers, but, sadly, wearing caps. They come, leaping and running down, with the stride of wild animals, and in a moment they are gone.

A horrible, spiteful wind blew. It was hot wind, and it sucked up spirals and eddies out of the dust and filled one's mouth and eyes with grit and sand. We were now standing on the peak of the path in the very middle of the amphitheatre. And rubbing one's eyes, and trying nervously not to swallow the germs of every known and unknown disease that must be swarming in this valley that was one unashamed and open drain, there was time to look round. The cave town of the Barrio de Santiago, this must be said at once, is much more impressive as a centre of human habitation than the sleepy, dull market town of Guadix; and as much livelier as Tel el Aviv must be than Tiberias or Bethlehem. Everyone in the Barrio lives on their wits, or on their madness, and of this, as we shall soon know, there is plenty. But the scene is of so extraordinary a nature that it must be described. I have said that it resembles an amphitheatre, but in fact, seen from the point of view of a spectator standing down in the middle of its germ-laden floor, the Barrio de Santiago is like nothing so much as a huge old opera house seen from the bare stage, an old opera house with rows and rows of boxes, for this gives you the effect of the different levels of the caves. But an opera house that has suffered in a severe earthquake, keeping the structure intact, but altering all the regular sequence of the rows and circles. Then it must be explained that the boxes which are the caves are often hollowed out of individual, soft, clayey dolomites, a peak apiece, or have lowered themselves into the earth up to the cowls of their own chimneys, in which instances, with smoke rising from their chimneys and with eyes for windows, they are often like the houses which become heads, or the heads which become houses, in Hieronymus Bosch's paintings. An

177

illusion that offers itself to the imagination is that every one of the peaks and pinnacles of the landscape round Guadix has its inhabitant, to which must be added, as well, the population who are living down below in caves.

You climb a little off the path and stand on a whitewashed platform, like a circle or a threshing floor, and it is, itself, the space in front of one house and the flat roof of another. Down below, there is one more of the white circles; the court of the house beneath you, and the roof of yet another. You are standing on the top of a three-floored apartment building; and walking a little further, the levels alter and you come to the cowled chimney of one cave, while, a few feet behind you, a whole row of the dolomite dwellings, like houses hollowed out of the huge ant heaps, turns a bend and vanishes. Across the amphitheatre, two hundred yards away, there are rows and rows of caves, all at different levels. The pinnacle or peak houses have a resemblance, too, to petrified tents or wigwams; and it is impossible to decide which are the more curious, the caves with their heads and two eyes or the wigwam dolomites, which should be cells of hermits.

We are in the middle of the first valley, wide enough to be called a theatre, but in no way to be compared to the full circle of the Barrio de Santiago, which we are now approaching. Other pathways open off to right and left; the wind raises dust columns which spin and move rapidly, like rainspouts; and tatterdemalion children gather in their swarms. We are climbing the little hill that divides the Barrio and that becomes, in symbol, like a mountain pass that must be traversed. Except for children but few of the inhabitants had yet appeared, but nearly at the highest point of the path there was a cave on the right-hand side, and this cave was a blacksmith's forge. We could see the fire inside it, and hear the anvil. A mule was tied up at the cave mouth, with the usual coloured saddlebags.

Immediately, there came running out of the cave an appalling mad child, a boy of fifteen, dressed only in a sack, running with an awful agility, like one of the clowns in a circus when the carpet has been put down and acrobats are coming on. He was like a clown running along very fast inside a sack; a particular kind of run conditioned by the sack that he was wearing. It was like the run of an acrobat before he springs into a set of cartwheels, but this imbecile boy did not wish to beg for money. He had only run out of the cave to see the strangers. A voice came from inside the cave, and he ran back as quick again. Outside the forge, near the tethered mule, there was a bundle, wrapped in a blanket, left upon the ground.

As soon as you get over the top of this ridge the entire Barrio de Santiago lies there before you. In size, it is as big as the largest imaginable quarry, but not as deep. The prevailing colour is white; the caves have whitewashed fronts, their flat roofs are whitewashed, and they have white chimneys. But there may be no other kind of town in which you get such an individual impression of the houses, even if, in essentials, they are all the same. That is why I compared it to an old opera house with row after row of boxes looking down upon you on an empty stage. For the theatre is so planned that from every box you can see the actors, and the impression given by the Barrio is that they can see you from the entrance to every cave. This is, of course, the accident that the individual houses are so small as units and that each has that one opening, if it is not a little square window. Then, again, it is a haphazard arrangement, depending on whether the soil may allow of a cave being scooped out from it or may have collapsed and fallen in. More curious still are the pointed hillocks, sandy, but burnt brown or tawny, excavated into caves, but clothed, sometimes, with a thin grass that imitates the dressed deerskins of the wigwam.

All in all, this must be the most extraordinary collection of human habitations in existence. And I say this having seen the troglodyte towns of North Africa; Matmata in southern Tunisia, a town with four or five thousand inhabitants living in houses dug into the hillside with a central passage, like the tunnel of a rabbit warren, and rooms to either side. Medenine, again, is of another type, with its *Ksar*, or keep, formed of granaries, or *ghorfas*, often of several storeys, and in the shape of the upturned keels of boats. Douairat, fifty miles from Medenine, is the most curious of these Berber villages, on a hillside in a landscape of bright coloured rocks. All sorts of troglo-dyte houses are in use at Douairat, caves scooped out of the hill, *ghorfas,* or granaries built outside the caves, and, as well, the many-storeyed kind. And there are the troglodyte Jews of Garian, about two hours' drive from Tripoli, four thousand of them living in circular pits fifty or sixty feet deep, and as much across, like great gasometers sunk into the ground, and approached by long sloping passages barred with heavy wood-en doors.[1] So much for the Jews and Berbers. But the Barrio de Santiago should, perhaps, be regarded as a natural phenom-enon, like the caves of Meteora. And if that be so, we have to look upon it as half nature and half the work of human hands, for even without the Gypsies the pointed hillocks would be sufficiently extraordinary. They would be comparable to the rocks of Meteora without the monasteries.

Perhaps the nearest equivalent to this astonishing individ-ualism of the Barrio, to this sensation that you are seeing every one of the caves and "wigwams" at one and the same time, is to be found in a town that any reader who fought in the campaign from North Africa up the Adriatic coast of Italy may have come across. This is Alberobello, forty miles from Bari, a town of *trulli,* round, conical, whitewashed houses with thatched roofs, unique in Europe with its six thousand inhabi-tants, for the only prototype to these primitive dwellings, which are often in groups (i.e. one house formed from several units), is in the *nuraghi,* with their vaulted roofs formed from layers of stones projecting one beyond the other, which are the prehistoric ruins of Sardinia. And the person who sees Albero-bello has under his eyes the living equivalent of the beehive tombs of Mycenae.[2]

How old is the Barrio de Santiago? For how long has it been inhabited? This is a question to which it is impossible to find an answer. There may have been a sudden swarming of the Gypsy population in the last hundred years. And why at Gua-

[1] Cf. *Mauretania,* by Sacheverell Sitwell, London, Duckworth & Co., 1940, pp. 307–309.
[2] The same neolithic culture excavated the rock chambers of Malta and the *sesi* of Pantellaria, the isle between Sicily and Tunis.

dix? Why at Guadix, more than at Granada; or at any one of many other towns in Spain where there are Gypsies? Guadix is not suited, particularly, for a big Gypsy population. Yet the Barrio may have been inhabited for as long as Albaicín. For five hundred years and more, beginning, no doubt, with the Berbers who came over with the Arabs, and whose villages in North Africa were not dissimilar to this. To what extent were there wandering families of Bedouins in Spain under the Moors, as now in Algeria and Tunisia? For the Bedouins will pitch their low tents by the cactus and the prickly pear; or crawl into holes in the rock or hollows in the ground. The outskirts of the towns were a refuge for robbers and bad characters, for vagabonds and beggars. They were outside the town gates which were locked at night. And the origin of the cave population may be due to all these things. The Gypsies first came into Spain in the fifteenth century, and it is reasonable to suppose that a few families would begin living in the caves outside the towns. At Granada, arriving soon after the conquest, they would probably pass themselves off as Moors. If they had to be Christians, they would be Christians immediately, and for the asking. Then, when there was persecution, the Moriscos would be weeded out and the Gypsies would remain. As late as the end of the eighteenth century it is doubtful if either the Albaicín or Triana had more than a few families of Gypsies living in them. The swarming seems to have come in the nineteenth century, perhaps owing to some elementary improvement in conditions. No more than a diminution in the rate of infant mortality would be enough to account for a steep increase of the population. They would multiply as the Indians multiplied under British rule in India, doubling and trebling their population in a hundred years.

But this does not explain why Guadix, in particular, should be favoured by the Gypsies. The beet industry could be described as a late introduction not dating further back than the end of the last century. So it seems probable that it was as much the natural amenities of the Barrio, as any other reason, that drew the Gypsies in large numbers to this town of caves. They had formed the habit, and here were the caves ready for them. I would even suggest that they stayed and increased in Guadix because the fantastic landscape appealed to them, and I believe this to be the reason why they inhabit both the Barrio and the Albaicín. Their genius is not content with the ordinary suburb of a town.

Such is the case, too, in other lands where the Gypsies have ceased to be nomads and become sedentary. The most remarkable of their settlements, outside Spain, may be Sliven in Bulgaria, an old town with Turkish minarets and snowy mountains in the distance; a place of old wooden houses by the banks of rushing mountain torrents, with a Gypsy quarter in a high quarter of the town, known by the name of the "Blue Rocks". This had been of old, a hunting ground of the Turkish Sultan Mehmet IV, where he hunted with falcons. It has limestone hills like blue dolomites, full of a blue shadow at sunset, where the Gypsies have their caves. The analogy of Sliven to the Barrio de Santiago is so obvious that it does not need stressing. And with this comparison I conclude my account of the most extraordinary collection of human habitations that I have ever seen. In thinking of it I have only one regret, that I missed the Gitanos of the Cuevas de la Vera. Yet more, the Gypsy Caves of Beralúa, five miles north of Guadix, and according to Dr. Walter Starkie, wilder still.

4. CODA AND FINALE

Bull Fights – Spanish Music – Finale

During a Feria, a bull fight.

I have lying before me, as I write this, the back of a menu upon which is written:

Pepín Martín Vázquez
Pepe Luis Vázquez
Domingo Ortega
Luis Miguel Dominguín

This was given me by two brothers (hotel proprietors in Alicante), and it is invitation enough. We find ourselves shortly before half-past five on a Sunday afternoon in some bigger Spanish town, paying off a taxi, and pushing our way through the crowd towards the bull ring.

There is no other sensation in the world quite like the arrival at a bull fight. A surging, indescribable excitement of the blood and nerves. I can even understand and enter into the feelings of someone who might go to Spain only in order to watch the crowds arriving for a bull fight. But it is close on the half-hour, and there is wild struggling at the gates to get in. We are on the wrong stair, and have to make a rush to hire cushions, and then we emerge from another stair out into the sunlight of the arena, "when the classical scene bursts upon us in all the glory of the South". We are in the bull ring of Valencia for the great festival bull fight of the Fallas.

There are persons standing on the roofs of high buildings overlooking the arena, and there are posters and advertisements all round the ring. We admire the few ladies, here and there in the huge audience, who are wearing the old Valencian costume; and as we climb into our seats and look back, the procession of *toreros* is half-way across the sanded floor. We had not seen them enter, but here, close to us, are the pair of *alguacils* on horseback, in their plumed hats and cloaks, saluting the president, and behind them the *matadores* in their *capotes de paseo*, embroidered with roses and carnations, holding their black caps in their hands, bowing in front of the president's box, putting their caps on their heads again, marching to the barrier, throwing their cloaks over the edge of that; and after them the *banderilleros*, only less splendid in array; the *picadores*, heavier in build, riding their poor nags; and the *chulos* or *monos* in blood-reds shirts whipping up their mule team.

The president throws down the key of the *toril* into the sand, and one of the *alguaciles* gallops across the arena and gives it to the doorkeeper. The trumpets sound a fanfare, the door opens wide, and after an instant a great black bull dashes, snorting, into the sunlight, and stops and paws the sand. It is not as big a bull as those of English farmyards and meadows, but more agile and with tremendous muscles about its neck and back. It is engaged by a young *torero*, who plays it with his cloak; meanwhile a *picador* gallops his limping horse round the edge of the arena, the long way round, and draws nearer to the bull. The horse, we notice, is protected at the front and flanks with mattresses and has its right eye bandaged so that it cannot see. . . .

From now on there may be a dazzling display of grace and swordsmanship, or dull slaughter, for we have not space to describe the bull fight in all its phases. Since the death of Manolete, many, perhaps the majority, of Spaniards will tell you that it is more likely to be the latter than the former. It was so at the bull fights in Seville during the Feria of 1947, and it was no better at the great festival bull fight held at Valencia in 1948. The death of nearly every bull was stupidly and needlessly protracted; sword after sword was put into the bulls without inflicting a mortal wound. With an artist of the calibre of Manolete the bull would fall lifeless at his feet after a single stroke. No *matador* walked into the bull ring as did Manolete. For Manolete was a great artist. He was of the order of a Chaliapin or a Nijinski. "No tragedian ever trod the stage, nor gladiator ever entered the arena, with more grace and manly dignity." His long, grave, aristocratic features set him apart. He was a "Roman" of old Córdoba. He was of the sort that comes but once in a lifetime or once only in a hundred years. And I never saw him! The nearest to approach him was the Gypsy, Joselito, killed in the Talavera bull ring in 1920, when he was only twenty-four of age. For the bull ring *is* a dangerous profession, ending more often than not in a violent and painful death, and the greatest of the matadors *are* artists. The bull fight, at its best, is as much a work of art as are most ballets. For myself, though I find it difficult to condone, I would not keep away from a bull fight. I would always want to go.

But there is another form of bull fight that I believe all fair-minded persons would acclaim and honour as a sport. This is the bull fought from horseback with the pike, *rejoneado*, in Portuguese style, that is to say, after the manner of the bull

184

fights held in Portugal, except that the bull is killed. But there is no recourse to the *picadores*; the bull is not, first, tired out and forced to keep its head down in position for the kill by lifting horse and rider on its horns. Instead, the *banderillas* are thrown and the bull is killed from horseback, and it is a point of honour that the highly trained horse or pony must not be touched by the bull's horns. This is a gallant and beautiful spectacle to watch, and I cannot see that it is more cruel than hunting, shooting, fishing, than any sport involving death to the animal that is hunted.

The spangled suits of the *toreros* are immensely heavy, far heavier than they look, in order to afford protection. There are tailors and embroiderers for the bull fighters in Madrid and in Seville, and many of their capes and costumes are real works of art. The flower embroidery of the *capotes de paseo* is, even, a style of embroidery of its own. To have seen the tall, lithe figure of Luis Miguel Dominguín entering the ring in his suit of dark crimson, or I would call it damson and black lace, must be accounted a theatrical sensation – to one who loves the theatre. But for full information upon all such topics we have recourse to the huge, and just completed, encyclopaedia of *Tauromaquia,* in three volumes, by Don José M. Cossío. Within its pages we meet Montes, saluted by Théophile Gautier a hundred years ago as the first swordsman of Spain, dressed in blue, a rare colour in the bull ring, but which flatters his tall figure, waspish or Minoan waist, and whiskered face. And it becomes a fascination to turn the pages of the *Tauromaquia* trying, for one thing, to compute the number of *Gitanos* among the bull fighters – and it is considerable – as in the number of bull fighters who have come to violent ends. There is the doyen of the picadors – now dead? – who passed his latter years as *torilero* (janitor and opener of the bull's den) and who is calculated to have witnessed the death of thirty thousand bulls, and by the same token, of one hundred and twenty thousand horses. All this, and more, is to be found, together with the history of the *ganaderías* (stud farms) and reproductions of their branding marks. The classical dress of the *matador de toros* is presented here in all its finery. If there be a regret it is that the bull fights of Portugal are not described in detail, and we could wish for more information concerning the *ganaderías* of the Ribatejo, and of the differences in costume between the bull fighters of Portugal and Spain. Probably the Portuguese type in perfection is the *cavaleiro* Simão de Vega riding into the ring in his long scarlet coat, heavily embroidered, with black tricorne hat and long boots.

But, also, there are bull fights – and bull fights. Hardly a Spanish town or village but has its bull ring. The national temperament reveals itself in the remark of a Spanish friend that she was looking forward to a certain bull fight "because the Miura bulls" (from a famous *ganadería*) "are going to be so fierce".[1] But the most exciting and picturesque fights of all are those held in temporary and improvised bull rings. I have been told of a *corrida* held in the courtyard of the Parador of Oropesa (the former castle of the Duke of Frias). Manolete fought on this occasion, and it was attended by the country folk of Lagartera, and of four of five nearby villages, wearing their gala costumes. In many towns and villages the chief square or *plaza* is turned into a bull ring for special occasions. Farm carts and motorcars are used to block the side streets; or a wooden stockade is set up with a space below it from which the heads and shoulders of half the male population are soon emerging. A famous *corrida* of this sort takes place every year in Chinchón, a small town thirty or forty miles from Madrid; while, at another town, the bull is secured to a post and balls of burning pitch are fixed on the points of its horns. The bull is then released and allowed to run wild through the streets.

But the most extraordinary of these pagan entertainments take place at Pamplona, in Navarre, during the Feria de San Fermín (7th to 12th July), when ten or twelve bulls are let loose in the streets and are "taken on" by the young male population, while women and children and older men look down from balconies and windows. After being driven through

1 It was a bull of the Miura breed that caused the death of Manolete in the bull ring at Linares. And a dead bull, at that, which killed Manolete with a reflex action of its horns.

the streets the usual *corrida* takes place later in the day. Nor must we omit to mention other scenes and occasions; such as the *corrida* held in Madrid, last summer, when the three most famous Gypsy matadors, Cagancho, Albaicín, and Gitanillo de Triana, fought, all dressed in white and silver to show off their tawny Indian skins; or the private bull ring attached to the open end of the dining-room at the country house or *ranche* where the famous Belmonte lives in retirement.

Upon all such occasions, and it is not only in our imagination, we hear Spanish music playing in the background. Now there are many and various ways in which to apprehend for the first time the adjective "Spanish" and the meaning of the word "Spain". It may come to an Englishman, historically, through the coupling of the words "Spanish" and "Armada". Or it may come through music, and the love for Spanish music can be born in the circus or the music hall. That is the school in which to hear the most famous of the *pasodobles* or quick marches, and it may be many years later before we discover that Bizet was a Frenchman, not a Spaniard, and that his music is not popular with Spaniards or accepted by them as typical of Spain.

Nevertheless, no Spanish music whatever, be it by Albéniz, by Granados, or by Falla, is as Spanish as the crowd-motif from Carmen. And that is a quick march, a *pasodoble*, written by a Frenchman who had never been to Spain. A *marcha torera*, by all means, but we would call it the pattern of the *paseo*, "a sort of promenade which serves as an introduction to the dance – the dancers merely walk around, but what beauty and fascination there is in the mere walk of a good Spanish dancer", or, we would add, in the parade or "display", using that word in its peacock or golden-pheasant sense, of a Spanish crowd as they promenade along the Sierpes or the Alameda. And Mr. Gilbert Chase, in order to bring us back, pell-mell, to Seville and the Feria, remarks that "the greatest of the modern Spanish dancers, Pastora Imperio, walked in such a way that it was said she had received his gift from God and out of it had made a new art – that of walking".

"Those eyes, those flowers in the hair, those shawls knotted round the figure, those feet that strike infinitely varied rhythms, those arms that ripple along the length of a body ever in movement, those undulations of the hand, those flashing smiles, and those Sevillian hips that turn in every direction while the rest of the body remains motionless – and all this to cries of *Olé! Olé! Anda la María! Eso es! Baile la Carmen! Anda! Anda!'* shouted by other women and by the public"; it is another Frenchman, Emanuel Chabrier, writing home from Spain, but a Frenchman who, according to rumour, had a Spanish wet nurse. Certainly, whether he tried or not, Chabrier did not succeed in getting the Spanish rhythms out of his blood and he was never more Spanish, at moments, than in his opera *Le Roi Malgré Lui*, which has a Polish setting. The valse-mazurka from this opera could be an early piece by Albéniz. Chabrier's letter from Seville was written in 1882, when wonderful, indeed, must the popular music have been, and the result of his visit was the rhapsody España, still one of the most effective pieces in the orchestral repertoire, never more welcome than at a concert that I attended, conducted by Sir Thomas Beecham, when it came at the end of a programme consisting chiefly of music by Sibelius.

It was at the Feria of Seville, or at such scenes of popular excitement and rejoicing as the Feria de San Fermín, that the real authentic Spanish music was to be heard, till recently. Let this be our occasion, too, to listen to it ! The Spanish dances of Sarasate and the pieces composing the *Iberia of Albéniz* are the records of such festivals, though in the case of Albéniz seldom, if ever, are they direct transcriptions. But Sarasate was a native of Pamplona, and he attended such festivals and noted down the tunes. Among the Spanish dances of Sarasate (1844–1908) so unduly neglected except for certain hackneyed pieces, sure enough, in proof of our argument, there are listed a *Jota de San Fermín*, op. 36, and a *Jota de Pamplona*.[1] If Sarasate calls a piece a *Jota Aragonesa*, it is because he

---

[1] Also, a *Playera, Peteneras, Muneiras* (these first two Gypsy dances), and a *Zortzico de Iparraguirre,* this latter based on the "national anthem" of the Basques, resembling an English hornpipe, and the souvenir of a visit to some festival in a Basque village.

heard it played in Aragon, but with Albéniz it is an evocation, the result of what he heard and saw, but sublimated, not reported.

There is so much more that one would like to hear and know; but it is time to bring this study of Spain, and of Spaniards, in life, and art, and architecture, to an end. In theory there need never be an end to it, any more than there can be a beginning or an end to Spanish history. And, indeed, the first and the last of Spain will ever be the same; from the walk of the *torero* to the spicy breath of the orange blossom, smelling of Arabia. And from the rows of bootblacks to the wide-gauged Spanish trains with hawkers climbing on board, from station to station, selling cheap knives and confectionery and lottery tickets. It is Spain, suddenly, in a moment, and as quickly it ceases to be Spain. There is no country in the world with so much personality of its own.

If you want to know this you have only to turn on the wireless and tune in to a programme from Barcelona or from Madrid. The driver of the motorcar in which I travelled over a great part of Spain used to turn on the radio, often when we were moving through one of the magnificent open landscapes of Estremadura or Old Castile, a scene with snowy mountains unutterably distant and aloof, like the ramparts of another, a lunar world, apart, a herd of bulls, or *toros bravos* perhaps, grazing out in the limitless plain, passing, as we did upon more than one occasion, a high, old-fashioned car with its roof heaped high with baggage, with its interior crowded with persons, to be told that they were matadors on their way from Madrid to the provinces and the bull fights; or he would "switch on the wireless" when we were approaching, and even in sight of, some old Spanish town whither I was going, if only, it may be, for an hour or so, in order to see the old buildings, some ancient town lost in its own obscurity, three, four, five hundred years ago – what did it matter? – and I did not mind the raucous or strident voices of the announcers, for, at any moment, they would be succeeded by the strains of popular music, and I would know that I was in Spain, and not just listening to Spanish music from somewhere far away, in

189

my own home in England, or wherever it might be, but hearing it in Spain itself, breathing the air of Spain; it would be in commentary upon that past that was my interest and in reminder that Spain and the Spaniards have a present and a future, that there are wonders, unborn yet, and still to come out of the Spanish idiom, out of that Spanish tongue which is spoken, alike by Cervantes and by Lope de Vega, by Góngora and by Lorca, in the Latin of Martial from Bilbilis and Lucian from Córdoba, by true Spaniards like Velázquez, like Goya, or like Picasso, or by foreigners acclimatized to the air and soil of Spain, like the Cretan El Greco, like the architect Juan Güas, or the sculptor Gil de Silóee, by Chabrier who only came on a visit to Spain, or by musicians like Bizet or like Debussy who had never been to Spain at all. Perhaps no foreigner who has ever been touched by Spain is ever quite the same again. Certainly it is true that Spaniards, themselves, are a race separate and apart, nowhere more so than when they are born to literature and to the arts.

Spain has within its borders some of the most beautiful and wonderful creations of the hand of man. There is nothing left in Europe, or in the world today, that can compare with the cathedrals of Toledo and Seville, of Burgos and of Santiago. If we want to know what was meant by the forces and wealth of Christendom during the Middle Ages we have to visit these, and look on in awe and silence. They are overwhelming with their loaded shells heaped with the carvings and tapestries, the pearls and gold and treasures of the centuries. The granite Escorial is still the eighth wonder of the world, inhabited, or formerly inhabited, by monks and kings, not a dead monument to the dead, like the Pyramid of Cheops; more awe-inspiring than ever Empire State Building or Rockefeller Institute could be. The "red city" or "red castle" of the Alhambra is one of the beauties of the world, hiding its courts of filigree and stalactite, its fountains and its myrtles, but the garden of the Generalife is lovelier still. There can be nothing in the world more beautiful than the cypresses, the singing or dancing waters, the roses and irises (an innovation), and the *mirador* (lovely word!) looking down upon Granada and the plain, and upon the hill of El Albaicín.

So be it! We have seen the "dark daughters of Moultan sitting in their rags under the vines". We behold them in their garish dresses swarming from the dark doors of their caves and pouring down the hillside. It is Andalucía in all the glory of the south. But those are the Gypsies, not the Spaniards. It is "the dew-dropping South"; in blue screens of cactus and of prickly pear, in whitewashed walls, in courts of orange trees.

There are those to whom such will spell false magic and enchantment, and who love Spain for her huge plains, and clouds, and snowy mountains, or for her cities. Some, again, love Spain for all these things – and for the Spaniards – who have stayed obstinately themselves through their long history, who are the same now as in the time of Strabo twenty centuries ago, now and ever, who hate and resent foreign interference, and who fire the heart and mind of the stranger with their music and poetry, their noble buildings and their proud and noble bearing, being, themselves, a part and an important part of the old and dwindling Europe. May they soon be bound again in bonds of friendship to their sister lands! Spain is a part of Europe, and Europe is not Europe without Spain.

NORTHERN SPAIN

La Coruña

Lugo

Santiago de Compostela

Santander

Santillana

◎ Oviedo

Bilbao

BASQU

El Vierz

Astorga

La Bañeza

Léon

San Doming

Burgos

Miraflores

Cisneros

Astudillo

Puebla de Sanábria

Benavente

Palencia

Bragança

Zamora

Toro

Valladolid

Tordesillas

Peñaranda
de Duero

Duero

Duero

Madrigal de Las Altas Torres

Salamanca

Segovia

Cogolludo

Cuidad Rodrigo

Avila

Guadalajara

Brih

La Alberca

Béjar

El Escorial

Past

Las Hurdes

Sierra de Grédos

MADRID

Alcald de
Henares

Montehermoso

Plasencia

Oropesa

Tagus

Lagartera

Tagus

Garrovillas de Alconétar

Trujillo

Guadalupe

Toledo

Aranjuez

Cáceres

Logrosán

W

Mérida

Guadiana

NEW

Manzanare

Badajoz

Valdepeí

L A · M A

SIERRA   MORE

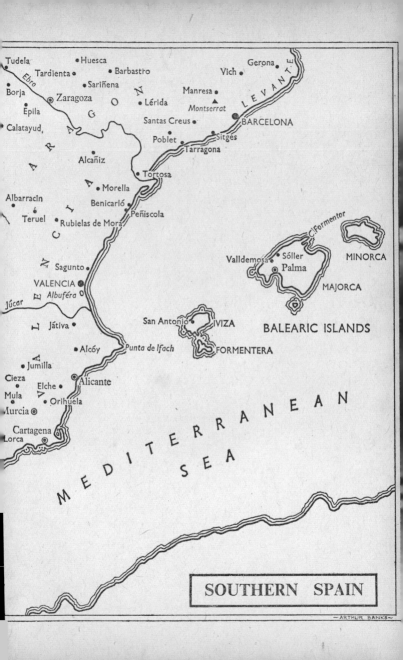

SOUTHERN SPAIN

~ARTHUR BANKS~

Index

The numerals in **heavy type** refer to the figure-numbers of the illustrations